KISS MY

WOMEN!

Take your past and define
 your future in business and in life

Kiki Rozema

 FriesenPress

One Printers Way
Altona, MB, R0G 0B0
Canada

www.friesenpress.com

ISBN
978-1-03-912799-9 (Hardcover)
978-1-03-912798-2 (Paperback)
978-1-03-912800-2 (eBook)

1. SELF-HELP, PERSONAL GROWTH, SELF-ESTEEM

Distributed to the trade by The Ingram Book Company

KISS MY

ASSets

"Brilliant! It's true, every woman can resonate with and relate to this book! I wish I had this ten years ago; I'd be a better person already! Congratulations on bringing this change to the forefront of our minds and for recognizing the serious need for a new perspective."

– Dina Morrison, School Psychologist

"Where has this book been? I love how the chapters offer tools and suggestions that make sense and are easy to apply. Kiki understands how women think and feel, and it shows throughout her examples and writing. I related to so many of the experiences shared, and that was imperative to my healing and ability to move forward from my past. A LUST read for all women; you'll LOVE it!"

– B. Schneider, Nurse, Mother of 3

"The title suits the book to a T. I love Kiki's sense of humor and her approach to a new way of thinking. Women's behavior towards each other has been the elephant in the room; we focus on so much in our lives that we forget how much we need to appreciate everything we are and everything we've gone through as women. I'm buying a copy for my circle of friends and family; there's so much to learn here!"

– Catherine Soares, Grade 9 Teacher

INTRODUCTION

Unless you're one of my friends I bribed into buying this book, we've never met.

But if you are a woman, we are deeply connected.

How?

Through the experiences only women can have. We are created to think, feel, and act differently than men. That alone makes us unique, and it makes us stronger.

If you're over thirty-five, you've experienced what it's like to be judged, critiqued, and likely bullied by other women, for your body, your choices as a mother, your choices in having a career (or not), and the list goes on. Women competing against other women has been a long-standing issue in terms of tearing each other down. We are incredibly adept at being sneaky, pitting women against each other, allowing ourselves to feel like we don't belong in a certain mold or fulfil certain expectations within society, and beating ourselves up for how our bodies grow and evolve through the years.

Let me share with you my experiences, my successes, and how I have taken my past and carried it (all of it ... the good, the shitty, and the misunderstood) to a place where I could evaluate what I needed to hold on to, and what needed to be let go, if I was ever going to feel "whole" as a woman, become who I was meant to be, and get to the place in my life where I was supposed to go.

How we "see" things, people, and most importantly, ourselves can make our lives something we either endure or (preferably) embrace. Allow me to show you how we can embrace our lives, with some swift pivots when needed, and an empathic approach.

I'm now fifty-two years old, and I want to change how all women feel about their bodies. I want women to work collectively, collaboratively, so we can succeed together. The time is now to make a difference.

Don't be scared; I've got your back.

There is no better time than now to look at ourselves and take note of where we are, mentally, emotionally, physically, etc. One of the greatest powers we have is the ability—the right—to reinvent ourselves at any given time. That gives us a great deal of power. We can change jobs, decide to be kinder to others, stop talking about people behind their backs, stand alongside another woman and support her goals and dreams, end a relationship, and vow to take better care of ourselves. It's all within our grasp, and I'll show you how I turned my challenging past into the foundation of how I now treat others and how I run my company. My life has not been something that happened to me. I look at all of it, the good and the bad, as what made me who I am today, as a woman, mom, wife, friend, daughter, sister, teacher, and student. And I know wholeheartedly that I can decide to change anything I want about who and what I want to be. I am also fully aware that, although I am a confident and powerful woman, I am also emotional, and I get tired, and doubt myself.

There have been a great number of experiences in my life that I still recall vividly and have not only affected me deeply but shaped who I am. While I will delve into them in more detail later in the book, here's a brief summary:

I have miscarried a baby (more than once). I have adopted two children. I have had two failed adoptions. I have gained and lost more than a hundred pounds. I have been through bad relationships. I lost my mom suddenly. I lost my brother suddenly. I taught Language Arts and Social Studies for junior-high-school kids for fifteen years and started a new career as an entrepreneur at forty-nine. My athleisure company is called Smoothies Tank Tops, and my mission with it is to change how women feel about their bodies and how they perceive other women. And I have also felt like I was failing as a mother and a wife.

I am here to tell you that, despite all the crap I've walked through to get to this point, it happened, and I continually choose how to respond to these experiences as they affect me.

If you have gone through any of the above experiences, I am sorry. I know how much these hurt. And I know how difficult it is to go through them and feel utterly alone. When people say you are not alone, does it help you? Do you still feel like no one really gets it? That's because even though we may have experienced the same circumstance, how we respond to it is always unique to us.

How one woman deals with a miscarriage is quite different than someone else. How long someone waits to take off their wedding ring after they've lost their spouse varies greatly. It may be weeks; it may be years. When my aunt got divorced, she continued to wear her wedding set for another forty-one years.

I hope that what I am about to say sits and ultimately stays with you for a while: We absolutely must remember that women are the toughest birds on this planet, but our own judgment can break our wings so fast that we can lose flight and drop to the ground in an instant. I believe women intrinsically look to other women for support, and all too often, we are met with sneers, gossip, and criticism. It stops us from wanting to share our fears, disappointments, and vulnerabilities with the women who are meant to know better than anyone else. It's a very cruel deception, and we need to change how we interact with other women, if we are ever going to move forward and feel successful in our lives.

CHAPTER ONE

GAINING WEIGHT AND CARRYING SHAME

I started gaining weight when I was seven. I'm not sure exactly what triggered it, whether it was a single event or a compilation of things. My first recollection of my weight being an issue growing up happened when my family ordered Chinese food in one night. We all finished dinner, and right after my mom cleaned up the kitchen, turned out the lights, and were all sitting in the family room watching TV, I wanted to get more food. I wasn't hungry, but it was like I *had* to have it. I snuck into the kitchen and stole two chicken balls, walking stealthily down the hall with them, not wanting to be caught. I went into the bathroom, locked the door, and stood in front of the mirror. Turning sideways, I saw a bloated tummy. I felt hot all over. I faced the mirror straight on and put the first chicken ball into my mouth. I loved the taste. Then I ate the second. My mom asked what I was doing in the bathroom, and I said I'd be right out. I knew what I was doing was disgusting, and somehow wrong, but my mind was telling me that I *needed* the food. It felt like a friend. I had on beige corduroy pants with a snap closure. When I sat down on the couch beside my dad, my snap popped. I tried to keep my sweater covering it so no one would notice. I was so full that I felt ashamed. This pattern of eating and then feeling guilt, disgust, and shame became a familiar occurrence throughout my life.

The most influential relationship you will ever have—other than the one you will have with yourself—is with your same sex parent. I hoped for a positive one with my mom, but growing up, we seemed to be on different sides of the fence a lot of the time. I couldn't understand her moods or why she was so unhappy. Even as a child, I took it upon myself to carry the blame for her unhappiness. It must have been my fault somehow because it seemed like she was always mad at me for something. Maybe she just didn't like me a lot of the time.

One Christmas, she got mad about something (I can't remember what) and threw our fully decorated tree out the back door. My brother and I couldn't believe it. We waited until my dad came home to tell him what happened. He just went out to the back and brought the tree back in. There was never any discussion about why she would act the way she did. I just internalized it and believed I was broken somehow. It didn't help that I'd been adopted as an infant. I added that to my list of reasons why I must be unlovable. Fifty years ago, when babies were placed for adoption, the adoptive parents rarely received any real information about the birth parents, or *why* the baby was being placed for adoption. For me, that meant a lot of unanswered questions, and my brain filled in the gaps. Our brains are incredible that way, trying to make sense of our world, but it can wreak havoc on our belief systems if we don't have the facts.

In grade two, I was in jazz, and we had a Christmas party coming up. I needed a nice dress, so my mom and I went to the mall to get something. I remember being so excited to have a new dress! We went into a few different stores, but nothing fit, or else it didn't suit the occasion. I hated looking in the mirror in the changerooms. I felt so defeated. Finally, I heard my mom outside the door, saying, "Kirstin (my full name), we just can't find anything because you're so big."

Dejectedly, I came out, and we ventured over to the department store, Simpsons-Sears. Mom told me to go into the changeroom and wait. She finally came back with a blouse with ruffles around the neck (so pretty!!) and a gorgeous emerald, green-velvet A-line dress. I put the blouse on. It fit! Then I slipped the dress over my head. *It fit too!!* I was so elated that I nearly cried. It looked good and didn't pinch my stomach, like my pants always did. I didn't even feel fat. I changed back into my regular clothes and met my mom at the register. I was glad she had gone ahead, because there was a huge line up, and I was hungry.

As I stood beside mom, the store clerk took the dress and said to my mom, "Congratulations! When are you due?"

My mom replied, "Oh this outfit is for my daughter, because she can't fit into anything else."

I looked around and saw all the women with swollen bellies in line. We were in the maternity section of the department store. The heat ran from my head to my toes. My face dropped, the tears fell, and my anxiety went through the roof. I was too fat to wear normal clothes. I couldn't help the sobs. I was so embarrassed that I wanted to crawl into a hole and disappear. We drove across the street to McDonald's and went to the drive thru. I couldn't eat; I wanted to throw up.

My mother said, "Kirstin, don't be so ridiculous! You're ordering dinner, and you will eat it!"

So, a quarter pounder with cheese meal was ordered for me, and I was expected to eat it. Right after being told that I was too big for normal clothes. I dealt with mixed messages like this for years. Years later, I wondered why my mom had been so hard on me; my perspective was so different than hers. I realized then that she didn't want me to be teased or hurt, but I had internalized it and felt unloved and unworthy. I think it's important to share these experiences with each other now, so we can learn from each other. Women have been too silent in our shame, our guilt, and our struggles.

The most difficult relationship I ever had was with my mother. The most powerful and complicated relationship of all *is* the one between a mother and daughter. I know now that she had been dealing with her own demons, battling mental illness, which no one talked about back then. I still love her dearly, despite her faults and her behaviour, because I know that she always did the best she could.

Did you have a parent who made you feel fat? Skinny? Not good enough? Not smart enough? Did you ever feel as though you disappointed them in some way? For the most part, I believe parents love their children and want the best for them. When kids have their own minds and ideas, they can conflict with the ideal picture their parents had in mind for them. I struggle with this already with my four-year-old son, Noah, because he is just so different from my older son Kristopher. I am trying to learn how to respond to him in the way he needs. For example, I work on not getting upset with him if he bites his nails. I think it's gross, but I also know that it's his way of dealing with his emotions. Of course, this sort of thing is another source of guilt for women: Why does my child feel the need to create bad habits? Am I not doing enough?

TOOLS:

Answer the following questions, and then try the guided meditation (link below)

1. What was said or done to you as a child that made you feel inferior?
2. Who said or did this?
3. How did you process this event at the time?

4. Were you able to let those feelings go, or have you carried them with you over time?

5. Our perceptions are our reality. If you can look at the events from a different perspective, you have the power to change how they have affected you.

6. When you have done this, consider the power of forgiveness. Are you able to forgive this person (or these people)?

7. ** Remember, FORGIVENESS IS FOR YOU, not for them. Forgiveness alleviates the weight of pain and anger, so that you feel lighter.

8. Make the choice right now to allow yourself to forgive, so that you can move on without those chains, which are preventing you from doing all the things in your life that you deserve to do and become whoever who want to be.

9. **Cutting Cords Meditation:** This is a powerful tool that allows you to truly let go.
   Here's the link: https://www.youtube.com/ watch?v=_Hm5aldk7us

   - It's important to recognize that parents make a lot of mistakes. In most cases, they don't intentionally mean to hurt their children. Maybe they were going through some internal struggles and took it out on you and your siblings. Were they awful parents, or were they doing the best they could with the information they had at the time? Perhaps they thought they were helping you, and just went about it all wrong for whatever reason. How is the past affecting you now? Is all this anger, frustration, guilt, and shame helping you in any way? I can guarantee you; it is not.

- Stop and consider the situation. Are you really a "bad" parent, or are you doing the best you can right now? Does the guilt you feel serve you in any way, or does it just prevent you from moving forward?

THE MESSAGE:
- Work through it and let it go!

CHAPTER TWO

THE SCHOOL YEARS

For me, weight gain/loss manifested itself as a nasty cycle of perceived failure. The feelings and self-judgement associated with being overweight played over and over in my head, much like anything else that chips away at our confidence. We often tell ourselves that we are lazy, unworthy, unmotivated, not creative, invisible, and yet glaringly obvious, and countless other negative things.

When I was twelve, I liked this boy in my grade-seven class. Towards the end of the school year, in May, I made the choice to starve myself. Each day, I ate only a single yogurt, some lettuce, a tomato, and water. I weighed myself three times a day. I worked out until I nearly passed out every day until the summer was over. I arrived at school on the first day of grade-eight, and no one recognized me. I had lost sixty-seven pounds in three months. My periods stopped. I got headaches. But I did not care; I could not stand being fat anymore. My best friend in the class, Peyton, knew my feelings for this boy, but apparently, she also "had to have him," so they went out, and I was left on the sidelines. I had never known what it was like to have a crush, and now I knew what it felt like to *be* crushed. And betrayed by my best friend. They broke up a week later, and I found it hard to trust her after that.

I kept the weight off for seven years.

Throughout school, I had crushes on boys, and my first boyfriend was five years my senior. I was fourteen. He wanted more than I was ready for, and that scared me. So, I broke up with him, and then other boys wanted to date me. This was uncharted territory.

How can you like me? I used to be fat! I wasn't used to this body that boys wanted to touch and look at. Teenagers are fraught with uncertainty, navigating their world. I wanted boys to like me, but I was afraid of what they really wanted from me. And deep down, I felt somewhat damaged from having been overweight. The stigmas around weight, body image, size, shape, having stretch marks … they all stay with you. We must make concerted efforts to teach our girls about acceptance and the strength of our bodies.

TOOLS:

1. Tell your children about body image and ask how they feel about their bodies. If they have a skewed perception of their own body, ask them where they see examples of these issues and talk about the importance and dangers of the media and its influence.

2. RESPECT your body and all it does for you. Notice that healthy eaters will carve out the time necessary to move their bodies and feed themselves the foods that make

them feel good in the long term (rather than immediate, stuff-your-face binges).

3. Figure out when and where your body-related issues first began, and work on changing how you see those early events and triggers. By doing this, you can change your current feelings about your body into ones that serve you.

4. Start off by making small healthy changes to your eating and your movement. Make a vow to create a habit of doing both on a regular basis, and don't allow anything or anyone to interrupt that (tell your family it's YOUR time). There is NO time for guilt here, my friends. Guilt serves no one.

5. Don't deny your body nutritious foods

   A. If you have struggled with weight gain/loss over your lifetime, you are probably aware of the physical and emotional damage it can cause. Extreme pursuits like bodybuilding are so unhealthy for your body. Body builders, for example, starve, deny their bodies water for competitions, and immediately after a competition, are so hungry that it is easy for them to gain weight in a short period of time. It's as though all their hard, determined work goes out the window. Cravings occur when we deny our bodies the nutrients they need to function. That's why diets don't work—over 80 percent of dieters gain back the weight they've lost, and (oftentimes) more.

- Girl's camps, seminars, webinars, and podcasts are a great way to connect with and learn from other, empowered females

THE MESSAGE:

- If you don't respect yourself and your body, no one else will either. You can't expect to have a healthy relationship with anyone else, until you figure out how to have a relationship with yourself.

CHAPTER THREE

THE DYNAMIC OF WOMEN FRIENDSHIPS

When you were growing up, did you have a best friend? Did you get into trouble and then laugh about it with the innocence of childhood? I remember running across the street with my friend Sarah, ringing my neighbour's front door, and then scooting back to the side of our house, as though we were getting away with the perfect crime. My neighbour opened the door and yelled, "Kiki? I can see you, you know!"

Oops!

Sarah and I met when I was five and she was three. Our moms met when Sarah's family moved in across the street. Our families became fast friends, and Sarah and I would hang out together when her mom would come over for coffee. We grew up together. Years later, through high school and university, Sarah and I would call each other daily—even though we didn't have cell phones then—sharing our boyfriend drama, weight issues, our secrets, and our greatest fears. I was Thelma; she was Louise. We even drove across Canada together when I moved away to teach. There's something about having a best girlfriend that supersedes any kind of relationship; it's that trust, that accountability, and the genuine cheerleading you can get from her. We've been friends now for more than forty-five years. We have endured babies, loss, divorce, toxicity, surgeries, disagreements, misunderstandings … the whole gamut.

But there's one thing that's never waned in all these years: Even though her own personal life seemed to go off track occasionally, there has NEVER been a time when Sarah wasn't excited for me. It doesn't matter what's going on in her life; she ALWAYS gets thrilled for me when I tell her good news. She tells me how happy she is that I have a healthy, happy marriage with a great man. She met me in Toronto after we brought Kristopher back from Florida, so she could snuggle him and welcome us home from the U.S. We only had a few hours to spend together before our next flight home, but she'd made the drive to see us. When I started my teaching career, and then launched Smoothies Tank Tops, she never doubted my ability or questioned my intent. We all need this kind of friend, someone who will champion us and be a cheerleader, tell you the truth when you need to hear it, and be the sounding board for you when you think no one else understands.

I find that it becomes increasingly difficult to create new friendships and maintain them as we get older. We become disconnected faster, and relationships can become disposable. I have a small circle of true friends. I've got many acquaintances, for sure, but my genuine friends are women I call my sisters, because we can say what we need to say, without it getting blown out of proportion, and then move on.

When you connect on a familiar level with another woman who has walked along a similar path, you can quickly become close. Take "mom groups," for example. The connections are based on motherhood, the hardest and most profound job in the world. When we can bitch about the hardships and idiosyncrasies of our kids and partners, it helps to relieve stress. We feel heard, understood, and accepted—not judged. Unfortunately, a group of women can have true bonding one night, and once the group separates at the end of the get-together, some of those women will talk about the others. People do it. But it sucks being on the receiving end of that, and it literally weighs you down. The energy you carry (and are surrounded by) becomes toxic. What do we hope to gain by talking about other women? You don't have to agree with how they discipline their kids, how many activities their kids are signed up for, whether they breastfeed or use formula, if they use Botox, or if they brush their chiclets twice a day. That's just you wanting to have your opinions validated. And it's worse when we are in bad places in our lives emotionally. Attacking another woman doesn't put you in a healthier place; it just keeps you in the whirlpool of crap.

TOOLS:

1. Use every opportunity to STOP jumping on the bitch-wagon, and try diverting the conversation, or pointing out something positive about the person being discussed. Share an experience you had with them that shows everyone else their strengths and why you're friends with

them. Share their value, instead of their shortcomings (you know, since we ALL have them!).

2. Female friendships must be taken seriously. Interview people and see if they are compatible with you (at the park, on a walk, when you're introduced to someone new at a friend's house, etc.). It can be a normal conversation but have it with a specific purpose in mind: to find out if the two of you really mesh. Ask the right questions to really learn about them. Share things about yourself that they can react to in an informative way. You shouldn't just throw yourself into a friendship and hope for the best. If you're not compatible, you will just have to break up with them like a bad boyfriend. It won't last, and you could end up feeling bitter and finding it hard to trust again. So be trusting and open, but don't share everything all at once.

THE MESSAGE:

- Female friendships can hold incredible power. Look for female friendships with women you can bond and communicate with, women who don't rip other women apart, who are happy for others and for YOU, and are interested in your problems. Find yourself friends who will understand where you're coming from, and who know how to forgive.

CHAPTER FOUR

PERCEPTION AND REALITY

In September of 1988, I entered my first year at the University of Guelph weighing 147 pounds. By Thanksgiving in October, I had gained twenty-seven pounds. When I got home, my brother Morgan said, "You look like you've gained a lot of weight. Is everything okay?" I got defensive and ate more to try and relieve my stress.

University was a four-year shitshow for me. I had so much anxiety about learning, being away from home, being a number in a crowd of thousands, and trying to fit in. So, I drank. A lot. I rarely went to class; in fact, my eight thirty a.m. Philosophy of Women class was almost a figment of my imagination. I showed up mid-October to my first class (hungover), and when I sat down, the person behind me said I must be in the wrong class. I asked her if it was in fact Philosophy of Women and she said, "Well yeah, but you've never been here before. Have you?" "Nope!" I replied. She leaned in and told me that I should make a quick exit, because it was the mid-term. *Oh ... wicked,* I thought. But I wrote the exam anyway and managed to pass.

My parents paid for my first year, and I didn't have the respect I needed at the time to appreciate all they had done for me. I felt like I was in survival mode. My stomach was in knots all day, every day. I always thought I was the only person who felt that way and couldn't define it. (I later found out it was generalized anxiety disorder.)

When I went home for breaks, my mom would be happy to see me, but each time, about a day before I was to head back, she would get mad at me for some reason, and I would leave to go back to school while in the middle of a fight with her, in a state of uncertainty and anxiety. It took me years to understand why she was like that. It turns out, she hated feeling "left," and it was easier for her to be mad when I left than emotional.

The relationship between us affected me on so many levels. It shook and ultimately destroyed my self-confidence. I had friends who used me, because I was so needy. I truly loved my friends, but I seemed to choose the wrong ones a lot of the time, and when push came to shove, my feelings were overlooked.

I did things to be liked, not respected. Being liked superseded anything else, and I tried extremely hard to win over friends and people in general. But my anxiety would often get the best of me when I got a job. I was so nervous and knotted up that I couldn't focus properly. I would get a job and then quit because the anxiety was too much to handle. I couldn't vocalize my thoughts or physical symptoms because I had felt them for so long that I thought it was normal for me. I would have to work ten times harder to get through life, pretending to be something or someone I wasn't. I had no idea who I really was; I tried to be everything to everybody, and it fractured my soul. I knew I loved certain things but couldn't commit. I knew I wanted to be a teacher but couldn't get into Teacher's College at first (you needed an 84 percent average, and with my poor attendance and lack of focus, my marks were abysmal). I started to wonder if I was really that smart. I found studying next to impossible; I couldn't retain any information and would do horribly on multiple-choice tests.

Life continued pretty much the same for the next three years of my degree, and by the time I graduated in 1992, I had gained upwards of ninety pounds.

When I finally graduated from teacher's college, my mom told me to lose weight, because no one would hire an overweight teacher, and no one would take me seriously. I wanted to wear cool outfits and be cute, but even jeans were a nightmare for me. Looking back now, I realize that jeans were made for a certain body type; and mine did not fit that "box," even when I was thin. I couldn't wrap my head around the fact that jeans were *always* tight in the waist. To me, that meant I was fat. It's amazing how we listen to the voice inside our head that tells us we are "less than." Women carry these burdens, these messages, throughout adulthood, and it stops us from moving in directions we might have wanted to go, like into a new relationship, out of a toxic friendship, or embarking on a career.

When I was so thin that my collar bones and hip bones protruded, I still couldn't wear jeans that didn't leave impressions around my waist; they were always too tight, with the legs and butt being too big. I couldn't win. I had convinced myself that, if a guy didn't like me, it was because I was fat. It didn't matter how many people told me I was pretty, or that I looked great; I had that albatross hanging from me, weighing me down. It's what *we believe about ourselves* that rings true. It's imperative that we are aware of what we tell ourselves, and because we have such a great influence on our daughters, we must watch what we say about ourselves in front of them, encouraging girls to embrace their bodies and nurture their brains.

It took me well into my thirties to realize that my weight had nothing to do with my lack of boyfriends. It was my insecurity and low self-esteem that drove people away. The neediness became my downfall. I thought my secrets were hidden, but I was wrong.

Why are we so brutal on our bodies? Women are infamous for hating their bodies and ultimately avoiding what it takes to keep themselves healthy. Society throws images of impossibly thin females, which we ultimately compare ourselves to. Have you ever been with friends who constantly bring attention to their perceived faults, complaining about their bodies? Here's a question: If they hadn't drawn so much attention to themselves, would you have really noticed their thighs? When you share how much you hate your body, it is an invitation for others to treat you with disrespect as well. We teach others how to treat us! Start respecting your body, and others will too. How do we reconnect with our bodies and learn to appreciate our shape and size?

TOOLS:

1. Meditation

   This allows you to sit with your thoughts and body for a period of time. We are in an era where things must come instantaneously. We expect results now. Meditation is not hard; you can download some incredible apps to help guide you through, if you aren't comfortable doing it on your own. When you meditate, it allows you to quiet your mind and body—both are needed to "check in" with yourself. During this time, you will feel any aches in your body, which you can identify rather than ignoring. In terms of your emotional and mental well-being, this time invites you to see where you are at. Are you in need of something? Once you start meditating, you will realize how much you love it, because you are claiming your space and time! This is yours, and you will become fiercely protective of this alone time. We are used to blindly going through the day, just existing, and we have left our self-care at the bottom of the to-do list. If you don't claim your time to reset, you are at risk of compromising your relationships with everyone.

   Do not forget, the most important and intimate relationship you will ever have is the one you have with YOU. So, speak to yourself as you would your best friend. You may not realize it right now, but you ARE your best friend. Would you tell your best friend her dimpled thighs are ugly? Or that she shouldn't be in a healthy relationship because of them? Or that she isn't worth loving? Do you love your best friend or daughter even though she is imperfect? Do you allow her flaws to interfere with your love and affection for her?

Have a look at this image. Where do you fit on this inverted cone? This represents your energy and where your vibrations are. It's very common to be sitting at the bottom of the cone, or close to it. Once you can quiet your mind and connect with your thoughts, etc., you will start to move up the cone and feel so much better.

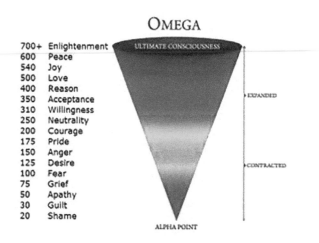

OMEGA

700+	Enlightenment
600	Peace
540	Joy
500	Love
400	Reason
350	Acceptance
310	Willingness
250	Neutrality
200	Courage
175	Pride
150	Anger
125	Desire
100	Fear
75	Grief
50	Apathy
30	Guilt
20	Shame

ULTIMATE CONSCIOUSNESS

EXPANDED

CONTRACTED

ALPHA POINT

When you interact with a child who is hurt, is your tone sympathetic? Do you have empathy for your child (or someone else's) when they are crying or in pain? How have *you* been hurt? If you could talk to yourself as a child, back when someone hurt you, what would you say to her? Would you hug her and tell her it's going to be alright and that she is loved?

From this moment on, you are allowed to speak to that little girl inside you who has experienced hurt, or judgment, who was belittled and bullied, teased, and felt unheard. You will listen to her inner voice and her body signals and treat them like they are your own ... because they are. You have the power to change HOW you respond to those experiences that have held you back all these years and continue to invade your mental and emotional space.

2. Yoga

   Compassion. Authenticity. Care. Empathy. Sympathy. Love. Respect. Trust.

   Yin yoga is the holding of poses for an extended period. The brilliance here is that you are sitting quietly ... listening to your body and feeling the deep stretches. This connects your mind to your body, because you are touching, moving, and stretching it. After a Yin yoga practice, you may feel tired, emotional, relaxed, etc. Why do people get emotional after physical exercise? I believe it's because we are waking up our bodies, and when we must "feel" them, emotionally, many feelings come rushing to the surface. Boot camps, requiring you to push your body to its limits, are often where you will find people crying. It is a great release.

   Why are women resistant to accept and embrace self-care? Do you feel like you have nothing left at the end of the day? Are you busy taking care of everyone else around you? The difference between men and women is huge. We are physiologically different, and we must be. It's okay to embrace those differences and not apologize for being hormonal, emotional, sensitive, etc. Have you ever seen a man try to multitask? Well, let me assure you, it's not pretty! They fumble about, losing track of what they were supposed to do, and get frustrated. Meanwhile, we are left holding the responsibilities of a daily to-do list a mile long. It's what we are expected to do, every day. We move from day to day, overseeing the house, pets, children, extended family, shopping, and work outside the home as well. (In the last ten years, there has been a massive increase in women working outside of the home.)

THE MESSAGE:

- Find some audio meditations on YouTube. There are tons. Find one that feels right for you. An unusual or grating voice can throw me off, so I must look a little longer to find the one for me. I often listen to mediations while I sleep.
- Wear headphones to block out any external noise
- Make sure you're in a space where you won't be interrupted or disturbed.
- Meditation can take place at any time during the day; I like to meditate at night, so I sleep more restfully. I feel significantly better overall when I do meditate. It is an amazing way to reconnect with yourself and learn how to respect your mind and body.

CHAPTER FIVE

CONFIDENCE: WHAT DOES IT LOOK/ FEEL/SOUND LIKE TO YOU?

As you are fully aware, confidence plays a major role in our lives. How do you view the world, and how do others perceive you? When we go out into the world, we typically have our game face on. When I used to teach, the second I walked into the school, I was "on" until I left at the end of the day. I once had a colleague (who had been teaching for eighteen years) ask me how I had such amazing classroom-management skills, which was something he struggled with. I told him to stop trying to win the kids over; he just needed to be himself. He would stand in the hallway with a hand puppet and talk to the kids—they were in grades seven, eight, and nine. He just didn't know how to connect with them. I told him to treat them with respect and talk to them, not AT them. And to be genuinely interested in who they were. But it just wasn't him. Eventually, I suggested he come into my classroom and watch for a few teaching blocks.

Afterward he said, "Kiki, I don't know how you do it, but I just don't have that THING you do." There is no magic here. Being someone who is doing the right thing for the right reasons never fails. Teaching is intrinsic. When I first arrived in a new province, away from all my family and friends, I was terrified. I was a brand-new teacher and didn't know the ropes in my new school. I asked other teachers for help, but they were very protective of their ideas, projects, and lesson plans. It made no sense to me. Weren't we adults? I was twenty-nine, a late start to a teaching career, but I was ready. I loved my kids (students), and I wanted them to know that I cared about their lives and ideas. Junior high is considered the hardest age group to teach because of all the hormones, etc., but I adored the age and everything they were about. I often had knots in my stomach, but I tend to use humour when I am nervous, so no one knew how I felt.

I submerged myself in learning everything I could about how kids learned, and the psychology behind family dynamics and the effects it had on my students. I spent countless hours preparing lesson plans, unit plans, and projects. I had no TV in my apartment, and I did my laundry at the school. I found that being prepared meant I could handle just about anything, and it drastically reduced my anxiety levels.

As soon as I felt like my life was on the right path, I met my husband, Neil, in a line at Starbucks. I don't drink coffee, but I was on Christmas break from teaching and had stopped in for a warm drink. We started chatting about the long line up and ended up sitting down and talking for an hour or so. When we parted ways, he asked me out for dinner. We have been together ever since. Several years after we got married, I asked what had drawn him to me.

"Your confidence, Kiki," he said. "You are so sure of yourself, and the way you carry yourself was so attractive to me ... aside from your beauty, inside and out." And I knew what he meant, because I had finally found myself about six months before I met him. It had taken me my entire life to understand that my mom's behaviour had had nothing to do with me. My worth was not defined by the way she treated me. But I FOREVER wanted her love and her approval. It was something I chased and could never get it. Why? Because I have no control over someone else's behaviour. I had to learn to separate myself from it.

HOW DO I GET CONFIDENCE?

TOOLS:

It takes effort. It takes time. It usually takes both emotional and mental energy to build your confidence from the inside out ... but once you do, NOTHING will break it. It can be shaken, and you may lose a few bricks along the way, but your path is solid and will always lead you to your destination. It also takes trusting in and surrendering to the universe.

Take some paper and a pen and go to your mirror. Write down what you see. How does it make you feel? Write it down and "sit" with these feelings for a while. Examine why you feel the way you do about your body and the person you see in the mirror.

1. What were your experiences like growing up?

2. Did you experience trauma of any kind growing up?

3. What was/is your relationship like with your mother?

4. Are you working in the career you always dreamed of?

5. Do you have post-secondary education? If so, are you working in the field you studied?

6. What would you change about your appearance if you could?

7. Why?

8. On a scale of 1–10, where would you say you are in terms of your confidence level? (One being low self-esteem and ten being very confident.)

9. Identify the reasons WHY you have placed yourself where you did on that scale.

Grab a large piece of paper and draw a line down the middle.

A. On one side, write a list of the beliefs you have about your body, your character, your life. Study it.

B. On the other side of the paper, examine the things you wrote and determine whether they are TRUE or just your PERCEIVED truth. In many cases, your perceived truth is the result of years of external opinions, ideas you have allowed to infiltrate your belief system.

The good news is that you can reverse the effects that those warped opinions had on you. And you can create a new memory path to walk your TRUTH. But first, you must be willing to do the work. The greatest reward is knowing you have built your foundation by yourself, and therefore, no one else has the ability (or invitation) to tear it down.

I've heard many people say that they can't trust their own gut, or they are so unsure of their own thoughts that they must seek the opinions of others to make decisions. This is one of the reasons why their self-esteem has been compromised. Confidence is an inside job; you build it from within, and while someone else's two cents' worth may be worth considering ... you don't depend on them, because you have the confidence to trust your instincts to make the right decision for you.

THE MESSAGE:

You can do this!

CHAPTER SIX

HOW DOES MENTAL HEALTH AFFECT US ALL?

Is your lack of self-worth affecting your relationships?

We often talk about beating ourselves up, what it feels like, and how we see ourselves as women. Has it ever occurred to you that the people you love are also affected by your lack of self-esteem?

It's not an easy thing to hear. Think about your relationships with friends, a spouse, your children, your co-workers, etc. Do they know how you feel about yourself? Do your friends know you are insecure about your body, your intelligence, your beauty, your lack of success, and generally not measuring up to everyone else's expectations?

I believe it's natural to share our feelings with close friends, and certainly your spouse; they are in your life for support and should love you unconditionally as you are. But there also comes a point when your insecurities start to weigh heavily on those you are trying to protect and love the most.

Think about how you eat when you're in front of your children. Are you eating the same foods? Are your portions noticeably bigger? Smaller? Are you denying yourself certain foods and then allowing them for your children? Our kids are extremely smart, and they notice so much more than we often realize. They tend to internalize their feelings and will mimic your behaviour. If you say negative things about your body in front of your kids or within earshot, they will start to question their own bodies as well. They get their sense of self through your signals, your words and behaviours.

When you talk to your girlfriends on the phone, do you complain about how you aren't enough in some way? You don't make enough money. You're not ENOUGH? Our own struggles can seep into all our relationships, because other people see, hear, and experience your lack of confidence.

I am fully aware of my body size and type. I am cognizant of how I speak about weight and size in front of my kids, especially my eight-year-old son, Kristopher. Just the other day, we were sitting on the couch playing a board game, and he told me he didn't want to join competitive swimming because he wasn't allowed to wear a shirt in the pool. I asked him why he would want to (we wear rash-guard shirts to protect us from the UV rays when we are outside in our own pool), and he just shook his head. I told him his feelings were never anything to feel ashamed about, and they were never wrong. I want him to be able to share his feelings with me so he has an outlet and someone who will listen. He finally told me he thought he was "F-A-T" (he spelled it out). My heart sank. How could he think this? WHY does my little boy feel this way? Is it because

I am a bigger woman, and he doesn't want to be like me? Did someone say something to him? Am I a horrid role model for him? I asked myself these questions and then started to fear that I was the cause of his feeling fat. I hoped I hadn't said or done something to model that for him.

Throughout the years, I asked myself these questions and then paused and thought about my relationship with my own mother and how it impacted my confidence and mental health over the course of my life.

My relationship with my mom was often strained. I tried to understand why she would act the way she did; I just couldn't understand why she would say she loved me and then get mad over something seemingly insignificant shortly after, not speaking to me for long periods of time. I was well into my adulthood before I realized that she suffered from mental illness, which was evident when she bailed on my wedding in the Cayman Islands three weeks before the wedding. At the time I just couldn't wrap my head around it. Instinctively, I'd thought, *Did I do something wrong?"* But now, dealing with it from a logical standpoint, I realise that it was never about me.

Something to keep in mind: When someone does something that leaves you feeling confused and/or hurt, rather than trying to guess what the issue is, just ask. If you still can't find the answer, you must move forward, knowing you've done your best, and it most likely has absolutely NOTHING to do with you. That is another sign of being confident with who you are. Knowing you tried your best and being able to accept that means you don't overthink situations or blame yourself for someone else's words or actions.

After my wedding, I pulled away from the need to have my mom love me the way I wanted her to, and did my best to be independent, rarely asking for help from friends, but often offering help to others; I felt needed and purposeful when I could help someone else, nurturing or comforting them.

Teaching certainly offered that sense of making a difference and helping others; it was an amazing time in my life when I truly felt like I was making an impact on students.

It seems to be in our makeup, as women, to blame ourselves for all the things that are wrong in our lives. We could always be doing more, loving better, working harder. Somehow, we seem to fall short; we fail society's expectations of what we should be doing and who we "should be." If our children are unhappy, it must be something we did. If our husbands aren't attracted to us, it is because we have let ourselves go; we have cellulite, our boobs are in another postal code ... the berating just doesn't end. And if we have kids? When we are so critical of our own bodies, what is that telling them? Parents of the same sex child have the most influence on that child. Our daughters are watching, listening, learning, and adopting our thoughts and beliefs.

On Thursday, February 15, 2019, I was driving to meet my friend, and the phone rang in my car. I saw that it was my dad. (My mom hadn't answered my calls in nine months, so I knew it was my dad.)

I turned the music down and answered. "HI, Dad! What's up?"

"Kiki, your mom is dying, okay?"

My heart skipped a beat. Had I just heard what I thought I'd heard? I pulled over. "What??" My world stopped.

"Kiki, I thought she was going to die yesterday, but she's hanging on."

"Dad, I can't talk, but I'm on the next flight out."

In that split second, every single negative thought or feeling I'd had towards her had been washed away. This was my mother. She was leaving me, and I had to get there. I had a paradigm shift in my thinking: I KNEW, in that moment, that she had always loved me fiercely, but her mental illness had prevented her from being able to do that freely.

All the shitty things we'd said to each other and all the hurt we'd felt, none of it was her fault. We didn't know how to communicate with each other, so there was a great deal of context that was misconstrued and misunderstood. The only way we knew how to navigate it was to put it on ourselves, in true female fashion. We blame ourselves, carry the pain on our shoulders, and put one foot in front of the other.

I sped to Neil's accounting office and ran down the hall, calling his name, and then told him, "Get me on a plane! My mom is DYING!!!!"

On my way to her, I called the hospital, and they told me she could hear me if I spoke to her, though she was no longer able to speak. The nurses were kind and put the phone to mom's ear. "MOM! It's Kiki. I'm coming. I'm coming! Please wait for me, I love you! I love you more than anything, and I am so sorry for everything I have ever done and for every way I hurt you. I love you so much, and you have to wait until I get there, PLEASE!" I heard a deep groan on the other end of the phone. The nurse told me she'd heard me, because she moved her eyes. I called and spoke to my mom three more times, telling her I was coming to hold her hand and kiss her face. I thanked her for choosing me to be her daughter, and that she was the only mother I'd ever wanted or had.

Eighteen months prior, I had met my birth mother, and my mom had been hurt by that. That had caused another seven-months of silence between us, with her believing I had chosen my birth mother over her. I hadn't. I'd just wanted answers as to why she had placed me for adoption.

I arrived at the hospital the following morning and saw my mother lying on a bed, her mouth open. My dad was a shell of the person I knew him to be. We hugged, and I went to Mom's bedside. "Mama, you waited. It's Kiki. I love you." I held her hand and kissed her soft face. I whispered into her ear and thanked her for waiting. I rubbed her hand and touched her all over. She was quiet, and I studied her. I lifted her bed sheet and saw a diaper. There was my mom, the woman who had done so many good things for me and taken care of me when I was sick ... and she was so vulnerable, lying there, completely still, unable to speak, her breath slowing, her soul slipping away.

Her entire life had come down to a hospital bed and a diaper. How was this even fair?

I told her she could let go, that everyone who loved her was there. My dad couldn't stand to watch her any longer. She no longer looked like she once had. I asked him if he had said everything he wanted to say. They had been married fifty-six years and were best friends. He said he had. They had talked, and she'd eventually gotten quiet and closed her eyes. She never spoke again. I told him to go home with my uncle, who lived ten minutes from the hospital.

Apparently, she had developed pneumonia a month prior, and a few days before now, she'd had difficulty getting enough oxygen. At one point, she'd told my dad that she thought this might be it. She was admitted to the hospital and told that her heart was giving out, but if she had constant oxygen (carrying a tank with her everywhere), she would be able to function. She refused. They told her she would slip away, but it didn't change her decision. They asked her if she wanted anything. She told them a blanket, some juice, and my dad. He arrived later that day, and they informed him of her wishes. He was devastated; he'd thought she would be going home with him. But for two years or so, she had been suffering from terrible depression; so much so that she often asked God to let her die in her sleep.

When I got there, her eyes were open, but they didn't see. It was like I was in the twilight zone; I couldn't believe what was happening was real. My life flashed before me, and so many experiences we'd had together. I wanted my mom to stay. I wanted us to start over, with understanding and more compassion. But it was too late. I had no control over anything, and I felt like I was floating in this cloud of confusion and desperation.

Why had I allowed my anger and hurt to supersede my love and caring for my own mother? I felt like a failure as a daughter.

I was alone with her for hours. I took a picture of our clasped hands. She had delicate hands. They were still soft. Her body was cold, so I rubbed her legs and arms, but I felt like I was hurting her, so I stopped. I hadn't slept in a day and a half, and I was struggling to stay awake; I didn't want her to take her last breath with me asleep. Neil thought I should go take a shower and come back, but I feared she would die in my absence. It was as though I felt I needed to make up for my entire life of disappointing her, and I couldn't let her down now.

I was so exhausted and bleary eyed, and couldn't think straight, so I eventually called Neil and asked him to come get me so I could have that shower. I fell asleep after it, and when I awoke at four a.m., my phone had seven voice messages. I knew. She was gone. The nurse told me she had passed away close to one a.m.

Mom passed away on February 17th. It was her eighty-second birthday. She'd waited for me. She had waited for her birthday. I then counted the hours I was with her at her bedside: Seventeen.

My favourite number has been seventeen my whole life.

The next five days were a blur, and I was numb. I don't remember much, other than that I'd had to dismantle my parents' lives in a few days and move my dad home with me across the country. I sold their van, emptied their home, sold off some furniture, packed up my dad, met with the funeral director, identified her body for cremation, paid off their debts, and flew home with my dad holding her urn.

Women do what they must do, because only they know how. My mom didn't want to bother anyone with her problems, so she never talked about them. Instead, they festered and grew with a vengeance. Those feelings and thoughts swirled around her, and she suffered in silence for decades. That lack of communication among our family changed who we thought we were and deserved to be.

We try to be all things to everyone, and ultimately, we come up short, because we haven't given ourselves permission to lean back and assess where we're at and how we should move forward.

TOOLS:

1. Don't apologize for your feelings; they're real, and they are valid

2. Find some professional help (a neutral voice if you will) to help you find some answers

3. Be okay with not being okay

4. Communicate with someone about how you are feeling (all too often we suffer in silence with our thoughts pertaining to post-partum depression, anxiety, etc.)

5. Share the information with your doctor

6. Get outside and get some fresh air. That may sound trite, but it alleviates stresses in the brain and releases oxytocin (the happy hormone)

7. Not paying attention to your body's signals can lead you to a breakdown, even verbally lashing out at those you love

THE MESSAGE:

You don't need to be a martyr! While you are a woman powerhouse, you also need a break and some support. LISTEN to your internal signals and body's responses, so that you are aware of what you need.

CHAPTER SEVEN

GRIEF/LOSS

Throughout our lives, we all experience grief in various forms and to various degrees. From beloved pets crossing the rainbow bridge, relationships gone sideways, miscarriages, accidents, family deaths, etc. In a short period of time, I lost my mother, brother, and four fur babies. Just when I thought things would get better, I would get slammed with another loss. I wondered if I would be able to handle the compounding grief that seemed never-ending.

I had experienced four miscarriages and grieved the loss of what "could be." It hurt physically, emotionally, and mentally. But I knew we *would* have a family, through adoption. I could feel it, and I believed it. And now we have two healthy boys.

On December 1, 2020, I got a call from the Toronto Metro Police. The officer asked if I was sitting down. My heart sank and I started to pace the kitchen.

"Are you related to Morgan Shaw?"

"Yes." *("Kiki, you should sit down, honey." "No!")* "What is it? What happened?"

"Kiki, your brother is deceased. We found him in his apartment, unresponsive."

"WHAT? NO!!! NO!!!! NOOOOOOO!!!!!"

I screamed so loud that I don't know how my kids and the neighbours didn't come running. I asked if they were positive it was him (he didn't carry a wallet). They were sure. I handed the phone to Neil and went into the garage, pacing back and forth, hyperventilating. I dialed my dad's number. When he answered, I couldn't speak at first.

"Who is this?" he said finally.

"DAD!!!"

"Kiki, what's wrong?" I told him. I said how sorry I was. And that even though I had been angry with Morgan for so long, I did love him.

My brother had died suddenly, and because he had no wife or children, I was expected to deal with all the details from across the country. The phone calls to the coroner and funeral home, the autopsy reports, police, employers, etc. And he didn't have a will. I wasn't sure how I would be able to cope.

My brother, Morgan, was highly intelligent, good looking, and extremely charismatic. He had a great sense of humour and a mind for stats. He loved playing games like Monopoly and Risk. Unlike me, who would rather swim in our pool for the day, he would stay inside with his friends, playing games and pouring over hockey stats. He had an incredible memory for actors and movies, something he shared with my dad.

It dawned on me that the only two people left in our family were dad and me. How was I supposed to take care of Morgan's things? He lived across the country. How could I support my dad, who had lost his wife and now his son? I had two small children, a husband, and a new company to run. HOW was I supposed to manage it all?

Though not people, my fur babies had truly been members of my family, so when they died too, it was even more emptiness and loss. I had a business to run, a family to care for, and expectations that wouldn't go away. I never really knew what "digging deep" meant until all this happened.

Women are built for life's unpredictability. We must be, or the whole shithouse goes up in flames! I put one foot in front of the other for days. One step at a time. There were moments I had to stop on the side of the road and bawl my eyes out, because I didn't have the time for a breakdown that was more convenient. I still have periods of deep lows where I sob until I can barely breathe. It seems to come out of nowhere. A song, a memory, an image flashing in my head

I want you to think about all the times you thought you were going to crumble. All the times you figured you might just give up. You want to crawl into the pantry and shut the door, hoping no one will notice you're missing or hear you stifle your cries of frustration and exhaustion.

One foot in front of the other. Literally. Although my mind is often foggy—my brother passed away just two weeks ago as I write this—I know I can get to the other side of feeling like

I'm in the twilight zone. It was similar when my mom passed away, but my brother died very unexpectedly at only fifty-two years old, so it feels exponentially more painful. I grieve for all the things he could have still accomplished. When he died, I hadn't spoken to him in two months. It happened so fast, and I had no time to prepare. Then again, I'm not sure we can ever prepare for the loss of a loved one.

Don't you find it offensive when people say, "Geez, it's been like a few months already. You're still grieving?"

Insert throat punch.

How you respond to grieving is how you will navigate it and come through on the other side. It never ceases to amaze me how much a woman can really tolerate. It's not enough that we can lose a baby; we also grieve all the "what could have been" scenarios, watching friends play with their babies, when it should have been you and yours. And we question ourselves. "What did I do wrong?" "What did I do to deserve this?" Or if you have a child with special love needs, "Why is my child different?" In these scenarios, I feel like we view our bodies as having failed us.

It is so hard, but please don't fool yourself into thinking other people "have it worse" than you do. Or have it better, for that matter. We aren't comparing ourselves to others. Doing so is counterproductive. Your hurt is *real to you*. It doesn't matter if someone else has "bigger" problems than you, because what you are dealing with is *yours*. How someone else handles the same problem is their business. We can certainly support each other by being empathetic. Just because it hasn't happened to you, and you don't understand what someone else is experiencing, does not mean you can't offer your time, love, and energy to help that person in their healing.

TOOLS:

1. Allow yourself to feel.
2. Don't apologize for a meltdown … ever.
3. If you need help from a professional, get it.

Therapy comes in many forms. For me, it meant looking at my mom and brother's pictures repeatedly. It meant talking out loud to them and asking them to show me signs they were somehow present.

THE MESSAGE:

- Grief is personal; it ebbs and flows (like life), and it has no end.
- Don't judge someone for HOW they grieve.
- If you ask how someone is doing, be prepared to support them, wherever they are in their grief journey.
- Respect other people's responses and understand that it may not reflect how you would do it.

CHAPTER EIGHT

FEMALE BULLYING

Growing up, I remember how groups of girls used to gang up on and bully individual ones until they cried. Groups of three were typically a nightmare, because sooner or later, one of the three would become the target. Rumours would start out of nowhere, someone would get left out of a sleepover, and then the gossip would run wild. Girls can be brutal towards one another; it's just the way it is and always has been. But WHY? It's almost an expectation that a group of girls will be mean and talk about each other behind their backs. Girls can be sneaky. Insidious. They can smile at you while swearing between gritted teeth. (Have you ever seen this? Nasty. I want to poke someone in the eye when they do this)

Girls are encouraged by other girls, and their mothers, to be competitive and make comparisons. It turns into this brutal cycle of looking at other girls and sizing them up, commenting on their body shape, size, breast development, teeth, hair... There's a long list of potential insults to be found and then spread among other girls. And then there's your socioeconomic status: Do you live in a big house? What subdivision? What kind of cars do your parents drive? Are your parents still together? Do you wear brand-name clothing? Are you involved in extracurricular sports? Do you travel? Do you have a second home? Blah friggin blah.

These sorts of issues have always been a problematic reality, but these days, girls face even bigger issues, with social media stepping in, adding an entirely new bag of cheese to the mix. Text messaging, social groups, posting about get-togethers and then sharing pictures so that everyone who was left out can see what they missed. That feeling of being left out is devastating. You feel like an outcast. It hurts to the core when you are young, thinking you aren't wanted or liked.

Frankly, it's the same as an adult. I ran into a former colleague a few weeks back. I saw her on the ski hill and asked how she was doing. She told me she felt like she was in junior high all over again. "Why, what's up?" She told me to look to her right, where a gaggle of women were huddled in a group. She felt completely left out ... once again. She felt awkward and knew from experience that she should keep her distance. If she didn't, she'd either be ignored or would pick up on some sarcastic remark made in front of her. I didn't know what to say, other than to tell her I was sorry she felt that way, and that we (as women) need to be more understanding. No one wants to feel left out, ignored, looked down upon, and hurt.

I was guilty of bullying, I am ashamed to say. I've been a mean person, in my childhood and early adulthood. I'm thankful not to be that person now. And I am aware that it's because I would have done just about anything to fit in, rather than stick out for the wrong reasons. I've evolved, thankfully, and my confidence is built from within, so worrying about being a part of the "cool" group really doesn't interest me anymore. I don't think we have to befriend every person out there, but we must respect them as human beings and as women! And if our children see and/or hear us belittling someone else, what are we teaching them?

There's always the opportunity to be better people, in terms of what we say and how we say it. Women come by competition naturally. It's no accident. Society has a precept of there being only enough room for a few, rather than for all.

Have you ever seen the movie, *Legally Blonde,* with Reese Witherspoon? The women in the movie see Reese as a wannabe. So, it takes extra effort on her part to prove people wrong. She studies, dresses the part of a lawyer, and still has to work at getting respect. It isn't until she appears for a trial in her infamous pink suit and dazzling accessories, and uses her voice, that people learn that she is poised, confident, genuine, beautiful, and smart. When she decides to tell her ex-boyfriend that she is better off on her own than with him, her true abilities shine. She finally gains the admiration and respect from her entire graduating class, as well as the professors in the university. All it took was being *"Elle"* to really make a name and place for herself.

Women are beginning to get sick of taking a back seat to everyone else's needs. It's why the number of women entrepreneurs is growing in North America. Women seem to have the ability to get side jobs to make ends meet much easier than men. Our resourceful nature brings about some phenomenal entrepreneurial projects/ideas from the debris society has created or left behind.

Social media has just recently introduced us to possibilities we just never allowed ourselves to consider, like accepting and liking our bodies. Yes. Even the wobbly bits and dimples! Imagine being able to finally embrace our stretch marks, to finally recognize the miracle our bodies are. More and more accounts on Instagram are inviting us to view half-naked women's bodies in a way that brings us to tears. We look at other women with compassion, empathy, and support, rather than the judgmental bullying that comes from making comparisons. But while there are women who are fighting back against judgment, there will always be women who fight just as hard to keep women where they've always been. It's a sad place to be when that happens.

It's not easy trying to find our way and be true to ourselves. But happiness comes from a contentedness, an inner place of peace, and the belief that everything will be okay. Ultimately, no one can find it or create it, but us. We are unique and meant to make our stamp on the world as only we can. You must find your voice and know what you value and believe in.

If we can impose a more empathetic approach to women on ourselves, and our daughters, we could break down our barriers and start to believe in ourselves. I no longer look at another woman and think she is better or worse than me. But that wasn't always the case. When I left teaching in 2010, I felt like I was not utilizing my education or my intelligence. I found myself telling people I had a master's degree just so they wouldn't think I was stupid. It was almost as though I needed to prove my worth, because I hadn't yet defined myself as a woman beyond teaching.

TOOLS:

1. Be very cognizant of how you speak to and about another woman; we have spent years in a role that meant women didn't accept each other as powerful, intelligent, competent beings, so we cut each other down before anyone noticed we were insecure.

2. Stand up for another woman who is trying to better herself.

3. Be the voice of encouragement for a woman who is venturing out as an entrepreneur.

4. When someone else makes a backhanded compliment, *call her out on it,* and support your friend! Then move on.

THE MESSAGE:

- Women go through a shitload more than men. It's because of how we feel and process things. If another woman is acting "bitchy," try to understand where they're coming from first. We know firsthand how hard it is to manage everything we do! Stick up for your friends and do your best not to get caught up in other people's stuff. Reach out to another woman for support and understanding if you feel like you're being bullied. Stand up for yourself, and for others if you witness them being mistreated.

CHAPTER NINE

RELATIONSHIPS/CONFIDENCE

These are three most important aspects of all relationships: communication, trust, and respect. When one of them is weakened, or altogether missing, it compromises the relationship. For example, communication. You've got to tell you partner, early in the relationship, if you want kids—not on the first date but when you feel this might be the person you'd like to have kids with. I have witnessed long-term relationships crumble because someone finally spoke up (after the wedding) and said they wanted kids. The other person gets a shock and says they never wanted kids. Kind of an important conversation, don't you think?

Communicating with people is key. It's why we have turn signals on our cars, flashing beacons on the ocean, lit towers for planes, twirling lights and sirens on emergency vehicles. When we don't share our thoughts and feelings, people are left to guess, and that's dangerous. We tend to assume what is wrong, and we put pieces together that have no business in those spaces.

When couples have been together for a long time, life can create spaces too big to feel safe, and the communication wanes or comes to a complete halt. Years go by, and people don't live together; they exist. And when the kids finally leave home, you look at your partner and wonder who they are and what you're doing with them. It's a common reason for divorce; people just can't connect any longer, and they've lost so much time that the relationship is now beyond repair.

You must be aware of your thoughts and feelings before you can begin to communicate properly. This is precisely why yoga and meditation have the powers to heal. They force you to push everything aside so you can "hear" your thoughts and "feel" your feelings. And these practices have been around for hundreds or even thousands of years. I'm not saying you have to become Buddha; I'm just saying that you have to be aware of what's happening to you at any given time, so you know how to respond.

I've watched couples split up after someone cheats. It's no surprise that the trust has been lost, and many people can't get around it. They are now constantly wondering what their partner is up to, and their lives become a game of cat and mouse, which is completely toxic.

Spending time around people who call each other names, yelling at each other, demeaning each other, makes me very uncomfortable. It's extremely disrespectful, and if you have kids, it's teaching them that this is how to treat another human being. It's unacceptable in my books, and I don't spend a lot of time with couples who treat each other that way. If they spoke to their friends like they speak to each other, they wouldn't have any left. Think about your employees; if they were spoken to or treated in that way, they'd leave and/or possibly steal from the company. How would you like being sworn at or told you were an idiot in front of other employees, your friends, or your family? It's belittling, and there's no call for it. Ever.

Communication also comes in the form of replaying and considering the thoughts that have been ringing in your head, whether for a few days or a few years. What are you telling YOURSELF? What do you see in you? What do you want for you? How will you choose to respond to those thoughts and behaviours that have held you back for too long?

Now think about whether the voice tells you the same things you would tell your child, best friend, or spouse. Is it encouraging or damaging? Empathetic or impatient? Now is the time to choose differently. What you say to yourself is as important as what you say to others, and so is *how* you say it. If you've beaten yourself up for years (like most women do), it's going to take effort, and practice, to ease up on yourself and learn to listen. After some time and continued practice, you will be confident enough to trust your instincts. Your gut. Decisions will come easier, because the fear of not knowing or trusting yourself to *make* decisions will no longer be a part of who you are.

How you choose to respond to the world is what defines you. You know those moments when the Universe is testing you, like a miscarriage? What did you do in those dark, lonely, frightening moments? How did you choose to respond to the situation? THAT is your defining moment, hun, and it's completely yours.

When you start to practice the art of trusting yourself (just as you would others), the world will feel like it holds more treasures than it did before, more than just the black holes of fear. There is a certain magic about our lives when we no longer fear our surroundings and the unknown. Having the gift of trust within ourselves allows us to perceive our lives as something completely new. Possibilities arise, and we have the tits to take those opportunities and run like the wind.

Example: Think about something you would like to try, whether it is a sport, class, online dating, or something else that requires risk on your part. Ask only yourself whether you should go ahead or not. Working in tandem with self-communication, check in with yourself to see where you're at. Make the decision.

That is practice. When you do it enough times, trusting yourself becomes second nature, and the need to ask "permission" from others becomes a thing of the past. You now give yourself permission to trust *you*. It is one of the most liberating parts of human nature, and it's a true gift to yourself. You will discover things about yourself you didn't know you wanted or needed (as well as those things and people you *don't*).

Think about the things that make you feel less confident than you'd like to be. Why do those words, situations, or feelings make you feel this way? Recognizing the underlying reason is key. And it's why you have to take a step away from the chaos and crazy so you can identify them.

I've learned something unbelievable helpful and wish I had known it in my thirties or even early forties. (Better late than never though, right?) The strongest, most influential, and dynamic muscle we own is our mind. We create power from our mind, *because we have choices!*

Think about your past experiences. Do they play an active role in making you feel negatively about yourself today? I want you to consider this: You are no longer living in that space or in that time. That was then, and this is now. You have the power to change how you feel about that experience, and how you will respond to it. *You Have A Choice!* You can *decide* how you are going to respond to the feelings that pop up when you think about or face that memory.

An experience does not have to imprison you for the rest of your life. You have the power to decide whether you will *allow* it to steer the trajectory of your life. Is that truly what you want? Do you spin your wheels and get stuck at every turn? We create self-fulfilling prophecies by trying to live in the child-hood home that was sold years ago. When you try to revisit the house, there's new trees, new siding, and the inside has been renovated too. That space has taken on a new life. So should you. Things happen to you. They shape you. Knowing you can choose to leave that shit behind and write a new chapter for your life's book is EMPOWERING!

When it came to boyfriends, I liked many different people throughout my life, and I tended to have incredibly strong feelings for them. I believe that was because of my intense and constant need for love and acceptance. I was looking outside myself to find it, and it never worked out. Guys would tell me they liked me as a friend and that would be it. I would lose weight and like someone, only to find out they like my friend instead of me. It seemed like I was doomed to be single forever, and I internalized it as me not being worthy of love; I just wasn't good enough somehow.

I looked around me and couldn't figure out how some women had these relationships, while I was alone. I started to observe how they interacted with each other and learned what I would accept and not accept in a relationship (if I ever had one).

A relationship didn't form for me until I felt whole. Before that point, I believe my energy was pushing people away. It was in this new, emotionally healthier place, that I met Neil. Very early on, we talked about how we would handle arguments, and how we would deal with being really pissed off, hurt, or disappointed. I was used to being on my own, so I tended to shut down, while Neil wanted to talk things through, so we compromised. If some sort of conflict happened, we agree to walk a way for a brief time, pulling ourselves together, and then come back to talk it out. In the thirteen years we have been together, we have NEVER sworn at each other or shamed the other person. He is my biggest support system, and I treat him with respect. I also have complete trust in him because it would fail if I didn't. He's never given me a reason to doubt him, so I don't.

Being a whole person means that you've got to understand who you are, and how you handle things.

What defines us is how we respond to our experiences.

Think about that for a minute or two. It's key. If I want to be a strong and powerful woman with influence on how other people feel about themselves, I can't fly off the handle when things don't go my way; that's not how a leader behaves. If I make a mistake (and I do), I make sure I apologize and make it right with that person, learn from it, and move forward. I don't hold onto guilt, shame, frustration, or ill feelings, because it's counterproductive and gets me nowhere.

So, how would you define yourself? Note that this is where you are NOW. Not who you once were, and not who you want to be. Where are you *now*, and what do you need to do to get to where you want to be?

The opinions and labels placed on us by others take shape in our heads, and we allow them to create a picture of who we are. As a result, we "see" this person who has been pieced together. How do we begin to build our confidence from the inside after years of listening to other people? How do we learn how to trust ourselves again? Remember, the most important relationship you'll ever be in is the one you have with yourself. Women often look to each other for guidance when it comes to validating their feelings. We are upset with someone for doing or saying something that really annoyed us, so we tell our friends about the situation to see if they agree with our point of view. Essentially, it's exacerbating the situation; it's not solving the problem. Your group of "yes, I totally agree that she's in the wrong" just gets bigger. If you have a problem with someone … go talk to them. And saying, "I don't like confrontation" is a copout. It's called communication, and it's not always easy. It may cause you anxiety, but facing it head on allows you to build confidence in trusting your feelings and instincts.

Being able to tell your friend that she really hurt you by not being there for you (for example) gives her the chance to understand *you* better, and the chance to share *her* perspective of the situation, so you can understand *her* better.

Think of all the times you reached out to friends to ask their opinion about something. Realistically, you wanted them to side with you. When they don't agree with you, how do you feel? Don't you want to defend your opinion? Essentially, you are trying to validate your feelings/thoughts. But in the end, the decision is YOURS. This life is YOURS.

You've made it this far. While circumstances change and the world evolves, you can grow as well. How you look at things (perception/mindset) is massive in life.

Think of a child waiting for Santa. Think of their excitement, the thrill of getting to sleep on Christmas Eve just so Santa can make his way down the chimney to deliver those presents! Hoping he eats the homemade cookies, and they weren't on the naughty list. It's the power of belief. What you believe is your reality, just as it is for that child.

You have the power to change your point of view (and reinvent yourself!) at any given time, but it does take work. We are a society of the here and now; we want results immediately. But for most of us, unravelling the ball of knots our life has created can take some time and emotional/mental effort.

Communication is the number-one component to any healthy relationship, whether it's with a child, teacher, friend, co-worker, spouse, etc. But how do you increase and improve your communication with *yourself*? Begin with self-talk. When it comes down to it, even if you ask someone for their opinion on what you should do in any given situation, it still ends with you. You are the ultimate decision maker, and you know yourself best, even if it's been a while since you connected. When I decided to leave my home and drive across the country to start a new teaching job twenty years ago, I didn't ask a soul; I knew in my heart that it was the right choice. I drove in my Honda Prelude, with clothes, a lamp (one of those cheesy ones you tapped to turn on), a microwave, and a tiny table. That was it. I didn't know a soul. I was thankful my best friend, Sarah, drove across the country with me, of course, and it was an adventure we will never forget. But I knew she would be returning home, leaving me there in a strange place on my own.

When it came to asking other people if I should do certain things, it always used to push my anxiety through the roof, because no one else can truly know what's right for you. I saw a counselor when my mom was alive because I needed to find the logic in her behaviour and accept that it had nothing to do with me. At the end of the day, I felt as though I was expected to arrive at my own conclusions anyway, and I was just looking for validation. Now I know I have that validation *within me*. I don't need to ask for someone else's validation or permission to be me or make decisions for myself.

A great friend helps us navigate those times when we are confused or hurt, or when we've lost our inner compass.

What does your best friend mean to you? I'm talking about the person who pushes you to think outside the box and isn't afraid to tell you your breath stinks. The one you go to for everything, and who knows your thoughts, sometimes even before you do. If you are blessed with one of these friends, it is a true gift. It's why we love our girlfriends fiercely, and why we can let our guards down and have a good-old cry with them. We can tell our besties anything (Communication), trust that our secrets are safe with them (Trust) and know that they have your back and support you, your goals, and aspirations because they (Respect) you.

TOOLS:

42 Positive
Affirmations
TO CHANGE YOUR LIFE

I AM DOING MY BEST

I CHOOSE TO BE
HAPPY AND TO LOVE
MYSELF TODAY

MY POSSIBILITIES
ARE ENDLESS

I AM WORTHY

I AM BRAVE, BOLD
AND BEAUTIFUL

TODAY IS GOING TO
BE A GREAT DAY

I AM TALENTED AND
INTELLIGENT

I AM FREE OF WORRY
AND REGRET

MY THOUGHTS
BECOME MY REALITY

I AM IN LOVE WITH
MYSELF AND MY
BODY

I AM PROUD OF
MYSELF

I AM BECOMING
MORE CONFIDENT
EVERYDAY

I BELIEVE IN MYSELF

I WILL NOT WORRY
ABOUT THINGS I
CANNOT CONTROL

I WILL BE KIND TO
MYSELF AND OTHERS
TODAY

I LOVE MYSELF

I AM GRATEFUL FOR
ALL THAT I HAVE

WWW.WISHUPONYOURSELF.COM

Jot down where you are: emotionally, mentally, physically, spiritually (if applicable)

Emotional	Mental	Physical	Spiritual
Examples: Tired, frazzled, frustrated, sad, anxious, depressed	Examples: Foggy, sharp, creative	Examples: Unhealthy, overweight, under-weight, sore, strong	Examples: Trust, surrender

THE MESSAGE:

- Start paying attention to your thoughts, your feelings, and your body's signals. Listen to them and learn to respond to them in a way that aligns with your core beliefs and values. Connect/reconnect with yourself, where you are and where you want to be. You have the power and the choice.

CHAPTER TEN

TEACHING AND BECOMING

I was granted an admissions test for teacher's college in 1995; I had to write an eight-hour exam and passing meant a grade of 87 percent or higher. I knew I was meant to teach, but I had reservations about my ability to write a solid test, based on my previous grades at the University of Guelph. Not only did I pass the exam, but I received the group's highest mark, 100 percent, on the written portion, and there were 193 other students writing.

When I graduated from teacher's college, there were no jobs to be had in Ontario. I ended up working at a hiking store until 1998, when I decided to move across the country and work in Alberta. I was lucky enough to secure a teaching position at an amazing school, but it wasn't high school, which was what I had focused on while getting my teaching degree. It was junior high, kids ages twelve to fourteen.

I showed up not knowing a soul, and it was tough. That anxiety was still there, and I felt like I had zero support from family and friends, who were so far away. I had to ask a lot of questions from my colleagues, and as I've mentioned before, most of the women on staff were very protective of their ideas, projects, lesson plans, etc. I was asking for help and guidance, and I was getting snide comments and few resources in return.

So, I spent nearly every night and every weekend at the school, marking, planning, doing my laundry, and creating my own resources (I left teaching in 2010, and some of my Language Arts work is still being used today, eleven years later)

When I first started teaching, I was terrified. I figured the teenagers would eat me alive in the classroom, so I had to adapt quickly and devise ways to reach and understand them as a whole group and as individuals. It's what made classroom management one of my strongest attributes.

I became attached to my students and wanted to know them as people. I wanted them to feel understood and heard; hormones at this age are brutal, and girls can be insidious bullies, especially online. So, I stepped outside the box and taught in ways the other teachers didn't.

One year we had a lot of rain, and a small lake formed on the school property. I brought several blow-up boats, and we spent our drama class imagining we were stranded on an island. I was so grateful for my administration; they never told me not to do something. They gave me creative license to do what I thought would make a difference for my kids. I got flak from other teachers, saying I was the "fun teacher," while *they* were trying to teach. But my kids learned. They remembered. They imagined. It wasn't always from a textbook.

At Christmas, I had the kids build a huge wooden box and paint the outside like a sleigh. We filled it with pillows and called it the silent reading spot. We decorated our classroom like it was a Chevy Chase movie classic. My confidence was starting to return; I was able to count on myself to create new ways of learning, effective ways to teach kids at varying levels, and to lead.

I was tired of living in an apartment, so I borrowed $10,000 from my parents and started building my own home. Construction was crazy in 2004, and I was able to build an 884 sq ft, two-bedroom home on a huge corner lot (perfect for my golden retriever, Odie). I finally felt like my life was almost perfect. I loved my job, had my own dog, home, and my dream Jeep. What else could a person want? But I felt like I was missing that special person in my life.

The housing market was continuing to show promise, and my VP told me I should sell my house, as I would make great money from the profits. I bought for $143,000 and sold for $280,000 (I decided not to use a realtor and save money), so I was able to build another home. This one was 1500sq ft, and had four bedrooms, a completed basement, and a two-car garage. I felt so confident in all I had accomplished. On my own. I paid my parents back and felt like a true adult.

I was working out, had decided to get a German Shepherd (my parents had one named Baron before they adopted us, and he was an exceptional dog) named Fozzie, and things were great; I felt like I was finally adulting, and it was at this point that I met and fell in love with Neil.

When I began Smoothies Tank Tops, I was terrified because of my lack of knowledge in the industry I was entering. I had little experience with fashion, fabrics, and the manufacturing of women's athleisure wear. I had to move quickly, but I also felt like I was blind. When we aren't fully prepared to take on a new venture, project, etc., we show up looking and feeling insecure. That ill-preparedness can make us appear "stupid" or as someone who can't fulfill the expectations required. So, prepare! Research! Call the people who know more than you and ask them to share what they know, read up on the power players, and when it's time, you will arrive looking and feeling confident.

When we carry our past with us, success as an adult becomes lost in who we think we are. It's so important to recognize that our lives have been filled with events, experiences (both good and bad), and memories all the way from childhood.

What matters is how we have interpreted and responded to those things from our past. Psychologists and counsellors are always busy, because we have all been carrying so much weight on our shoulders for far too long. That weight isn't always apparent in our daily lives, but it is there, in our deepest fears and thoughts, and they hold us back from being all we can be. It's true.

I know the world can hand us crappy cards, but you have to remember that we are merely *shaped* by our experiences. What *defines* us is how we choose to respond to them. You have it in you to be incredible. Choosing your path and deciding your mindset every day is going to make the difference for you and everyone around you. You have the power to make some phenomenal decisions in your life. Don't be afraid to make them!

TOOLS:

1. Reflecting on your accomplishments thus far in life can really bring awareness to the forefront of your mind. Sometimes we forget how much we've done in our lives! Journaling is a fantastic tool for this exercise.

2. Take out your journal or a piece of paper. Think back to a time when you helped someone out, did well in a subject at school, did well at a sport or acted in a play, signed up for an extra-curricular activity, spoke first to a new person, helped a child, hugged someone when they needed it… You get the idea. Write these things down and give yourself some props for being a good human. Know that you can conquer a great deal, and that it takes only you to believe that. Now GO GET IT!

THE MESSAGE:

- When we embark on a new career, relationship, job, motherhood, and so on, it's the unknown that can scare the shit out of us. But if you can rely on your strengths, intuitions, and support systems, you'll be just fine. It's okay to start a new career or enroll in university at any age, and it's okay to realize halfway through that you hate the courses and want to try something else. You don't know unless you give it a shot, so don't be afraid to take the first steps

CHAPTER ELEVEN

UNDERSTANDING AND COMMUNICATING WITH OURSELVES

Women run the world. That's just the truth.

We organize, plan, navigate, nurture, foster, teach, administer, create, design, orchestrate, and divide and conquer daily!

But, my beautiful fellow powerhouses, you are kidding yourself if you think your gas won't run out. Think about how far you have gotten on fumes. Humans aren't meant to function this way. Give yourself permission to live authentically, and you won't have to fight your body's natural instincts to live your life as you were meant to.

Women wake up, and before they've even allowed themselves time to really think, the to-do list is upon us. We're extraordinary multitaskers, and we have to be in order for our families to survive. It's almost an unwritten rule (or at least it has been in the past) that women are responsible for the day-to-day tasks of the household. The only problem is that, in today's world, women often also have to work full-time to make ends meet in the family.

Trying to please everyone all the time zaps our emotional and physical energy, but we become accustomed to ignoring our body's signals until we are truly sick and come to a screeching halt.

When you experience something that leaves you hurt, mystified, and challenged, I want you to check in with yourself to see where you're at. Do you notice that, when friends react/respond in a way you weren't expecting, you wonder if it's because of you? Or about you? Ninety-nine percent of the time, it isn't. It's about where *they're* at and how *they* choose to respond to you. That's when you need to either address their response or decide to let it go.

Oftentimes, they will realize what they said or did and reach out to share what they were going through at that moment. Ever been on the phone with a friend, and she says something you don't get? Like where the hell did THAT come from? Instead of assuming it's something you did, or that it's an attack on your character, check in with them and ask if they're okay. Then you can better understand the situation. That's where you should strive to be in control and in a position to hear and understand where someone else is coming from. When you are conscious of your own compass, you're more likely to respond in a positive way that benefits people rather than hurts them, yourself, *and* others.

Understanding yourself is how you will understand others. Give yourself the grace and empathy you need to get through and past the experience(s). Allow for its due attention and then move on. It *is* that simple. If that means going to a psychologist or counsellor, make the appointment and stop holding yourself prisoner. You don't have to give it any more power than you already have. You're worth more than that!

I know myself better than anyone. I know I need to walk the dogs by myself so I can surround myself with joy and fresh air. I see my golden retriever, Mowgli, and my German Shepherd, Milo, jump around and run like their lives depended on it ... just because they can. It makes my heart smile to see them. I feel so much better walking into my home, where there is usually chaos between my eight-year-old, Kristopher, and my four-year-old, Noah. I have more patience to give them, and more hugs. I can offer kinder words when they cry about something seemingly ridiculous, instead of rolling my eyes and calculating the years I have left before retirement.

It's *so* necessary to figure yourself out—what you want and need in order to function at your best. Revisit the recurring thoughts in your head and figure out what you are telling yourself. What do you see in you? What do you want for you? How will you choose to respond to those thoughts and behaviours that have held you back for too long?

Dieting. Are you like me? Have you tried to lose weight through a zillion fad diets and approaches? Let me think of all the ways: Weight Watchers, Grapefruit diet, Scarsdale, Biggest Loser Ranch for six weeks, starvation, over-exercising, weighing myself twice a day, no carbs, high fat, high carbs, no fat, books, counseling, sleeve surgery... I have done it. All of it. And where did it land me?

Feeling fat, ugly, unworthy, unmotivated, and thinking I had zero willpower. Let me tell you right now that willpower has nothing to do with losing weight. Nothing. When we try drastic measures to drop weight, our bodies are being forced to go against what is natural and eventually will fight back, mentally, emotionally, and physically. This manifests as fatigue, the number not moving on the scale, feelings of failure, and eventually giving up because you start to gain back any weight you have already lost and then some. That is your body telling you to LISTEN. That is your body communicating with you!

We have to try and remember that our bodies are a part of who we are. The tendency to disassociate ourselves from our bodies is all too familiar. It's communication that's key in keeping us in-tune with our bodies and minds. If we jump on a trend or fad to lose weight quickly, you'll likely join the 80–95 percent of people who gain the weight back, and those feelings of failure creep in again. What a vicious circle!

Girls are particularly at risk for eating disorders, searching for ways to be in control of their feelings, lives, and environment. Anorexia, bulimia, and overeating are all ways to try and take control when we feel desperately out of control. It is so hard on our bodies, and the disconnect is obvious when we either lose or gain too much weight. It can cause long-term issues, delays in menstruation, and mental-health issues down the road.

It seems as though we are constantly in search of a healthy balance in our lives. But is there really a balance in life? We want it but attaining it with kids is realistically impossible. Juggling the schedules of your kids, jobs, and events takes a master planner. And because women are superior in this field, we've got to change how we plan.

I'm talking about planning *your* time for *you*. That *must* become non-negotiable. It *must* happen, whether it's every day or several times a week. CHOICES. You can make the choice to eke out the time you need for yourself. The next key part is to figure out what that looks like to you. It could be anything, like reading a book, going for a massage, taking a walk, volunteering somewhere, etc.

You should know now that you *can* have the life you want, because you have the power of choice on your side. How you treat your body is 100 percent your choice. So, if you put crap in your system, it's going to run like crap. If you pour beer into your gas tank, the car will eventually stop running. When we constantly put the wrong things into our bodies, they break down. And it's a sign of something else being wrong in the bigger picture.

When I overeat or ingest the wrong foods (for me that looks like bread, snack foods, and pop), and I don't move my body enough, I am generally punishing my body for something emotional going on. I deal with the stress by avoiding this issue and eating poorly, because it's immediate. It makes me feel at ease again in a short period of time. Addictions are like that, with the need for instant gratification. When the anxiety arises, you reach for the fastest and most accessible tool to level out the imbalance.

It's a semi-conscious reaction. There have been times in my life when I ate a family-size bag of chips with dip and never blinked an eye; I did it while watching TV, which is an automatic movement between grabbing a handful of chips from the bag and shoving it into my mouth again and again until it's gone. I stop afterwards and think, *Wow, I polished off that whole bag?!* I then become fully aware of what I ate and feel bad. I am overfull and feel like I am out of control. Then I start to think I need to lose weight, and tomorrow I will start to eat the right things, but I don't like how slow my body is moving or how sluggish I generally feel.

It's important to remember that how we choose to respond to a memory can make a huge difference in our emotional and mental well-being. When something is a memorable experience, we can often recall the day, the weather, what we were doing, etc. at the time of that event.

Think about the things you hold close to you, a memory that triggers sadness, fear, or anxiety. Something that keeps you from moving forward. You have to make the choice to let it go and create a new association with the event. It truly is a choice, and you have the absolute power to make that happen.

So, I have never quite understood why women can be such vipers towards each other. What gives? Have you ever been one of those girls? I was. As I referenced briefly earlier, I jumped on the bandwagon and said shit about other women, because I was unsure of my own worth. I come across many women to this day who claim that they don't judge other people and yet are incredibly opinionated about things they have never experienced themselves.

I've been bullied. As a child and adult. I hated how it felt, though I still did it to others. But eventually, I stopped. I knew I couldn't be a positive influence for anyone if I treated other people like I was better than them, or if I thought they didn't deserve the happiness they had found in their life. Who was I to say or feel anything but joy for them?

TOOLS:

1. Take a minute when you are inclined to say something critical or backhanded towards another woman. Think twice about how your comment may stick with them for life. It's incredible how our words can strike us and leave lasting scars

2. When you say something mean or judgmental about another woman, you are bashing someone who has feelings, a past, may be going through something and can't communicate it with anyone

THE MESSAGE:

- If you are feeling judgmental, keep it to yourself
- Try to see the situation from a different set of eyes and perception

- Don't bully someone else. It's a hard thing NOT to talk about someone else behind their back because society has trained us to do just that. Now it's our turn to take back our power and behave differently

CHAPTER TWELVE

JUDGEMENT AND GUILT

Here's something to chew on: I don't know a single bloody person who hasn't been a shit to someone, in some way or another, at some time. We all are guilty of saying something we shouldn't have said or hurting someone's feelings. There's this thing called forgiveness, though. You have to make it right with the person you pissed off, or hurt, or to whom you did something that contributed to their distorted sense of self-worth.

It's not easy sharing that I had the capacity to be mean (at times) to people. But I also know that it's taken me more than forty years to figure out what the hell I have been doing all my life that would make me lash out at someone in anger or frustration. Admittedly, I have always regretted making someone else feel bad. It made my stomach turn. As I get older, I look at the world and the people in it very differently.

I have learned to trust how I'm feeling. I am so much more aware of myself and what my intentions are than I used to be, and it helps a lot.

I would love to know how many of you have carried guilt, shame, and resentment around with you. I am truly baffled by the sheer weight of the shit we allow ourselves to carry. Do you know people who create more shit to carry just because they don't have enough shit already? (I like the word shit.)

I have known a few of these people over the years, and I just had to let them go. I got drawn into their whirlpool, and it became a never-ending cycle of trying to reassure them that their world was not, in fact, falling apart, and that it really wasn't going to be a disaster. But some people actually thrive on this shit. I cannot and will not carry someone else's shit. Neither should you.

I believe I used to *find* these people who needed to be lifted and helped along the way. I seemed to be able to spot them in a crowd and would try to be the voice of reason for them. It took years of failed attempts with dozens of women for me to realize that I was not a therapist. Or a psychologist. And holy good lord, I had my *own* baggage! But it was easier to deflect my own insecurities, shame, and guilt by focusing on someone else's. It made me feel useful in a way.

But there's a big difference between being supportive of a valued friend and being the person who must "save" someone all the time. Honey, that is not your job! We all have so much to unravel that we just can't take on any more. I don't care whether you are married, have a partner, children, whatever. You are a woman. And that means you carry more than your purse with you on a daily, minute-to-minute basis. Remember when I said that our past experiences shape who we are? It's true. How can it not be, when we have endured situations that only we can? You have to get comfortable being uncomfortable with those memories, how you reacted to them, how you felt, and how you have brought every single one of them with you right up to this point.

Being grateful for everything and everyone who brought you here is a phenomenal start.

I was adopted at birth. I had the pleasure of meeting my birth mother several years ago, and we communicate with each other occasionally. She still lives in Nova Scotia, where I was born. I texted her the other day and asked her what time of day I was born.

"I feel terrible that I can't remember," she said, "but I buried that time so deeply; I can't seem to get it back."

"I know you did. So much hurt for you."

"Yeah, well I made my bed, but I'm sorry for you."

"Sorry? No. Why would you be sorry? It's something that happened. You did what was best for you *and* me. I hope you can let that shame and guilt go, because I love you for all you did. And you have carried this burden for far too long. You don't deserve that."

"I'll reply later, okay?"

"Sure."

My birth mother reached out the following day: "Hi again. Sorry I'm so long getting back to you. Got a little weepy yesterday."

I am broken-hearted for her. She has *never* told her family about me. Never. My birthmother, Barb, hid the pregnancy from her parents, because eighteen months earlier, she had given birth to my biological brother, and it hadn't gone over well with her parents. She had been embarrassed and ashamed, and it had brought shame to her family. So, she kept me her little secret for years.

When I first met her face to face, I felt she was a little cold. But that wasn't accurate. Barb was actually guarded. Her heart has never healed from having had to place two children for adoption. She has never forgiven herself, and it makes me hurt for her. But that pain, anguish, and guilt has woven its way into her cells, and it's so painful that she can barely talk about it. She shared her past with her husband (who was a beautiful human), and he thought (as I do) that she was brave to be able to endure that. Once I was born, she wasn't allowed to hold me. She later told me that it was like a piece of her had been snatched away and the hole left forever agape. I can't imagine that sorrow. Both my kids' birth mothers had the opportunity to hold them.

For what back-ass reasoning do they refuse a mother who has just given birth the opportunity to hold the precious human they grew and nourished, as part of their body and heart, for nine months? This is cruel. Fifty-two years ago, though, this was commonplace. So was having a closed adoption, which meant there was zero communication between birth parents and adoptive families. My mom had been misinformed about Barb back then, and so trying to find any documents or paperwork relating to the circumstances of my birth had been next to impossible. It was only when I reached out to an adoption agency in Halifax that I was able to find Barb (and she wrote a letter in response to mine).

Society has changed how we view adoption. When I was small and told people I was adopted, it was like I was the only one out there, besides my brother, Morgan. Now, with infertility on the rise and the increase in drug addiction, etc., adoption is far more commonplace, and they are typically open adoptions, where both families have an opportunity to stay in contact in an agreed upon manner.

There are still social stigmas, but women are becoming more aware of their abilities and rights. There will always be women who can't believe a mother could "just give her baby away." That breaks my heart, because women DON'T "just give their babies away;" they are broken for the rest of their lives for having done what they felt they had to do, for whatever reason. The parting breaks them. While some women are not emotionally, mentally, or financially prepared to raise a baby, religion also plays a role, and to have the courage to carry a baby and then offer someone else the gift of raising that child in a healthy, loving environment (at least that is their hope and promise) is an amazing thing.

So, it is unbelievably cruel for any woman to say, "Oh, I could never do that! How could you/she?"

Don't do that.

I've had several friends get boob jobs. They look great! I have lived with my small, point-to-the south boobs for fifty-two years. I'll stick with them for the rest of my life, I think. There have been times when I thought it would be cool to have perky, full breasts, but ultimately, I ended up with a diamond ring anyway. "Lol."

Women have dozens of reasons to want a breast induction. Why does it matter whether your friend is a B or E cup matter to you at all? Even if someone doesn't "need" one, in your opinion, how does it even affect you? Why do you even *have* an opinion? It doesn't concern you.

Why do women have to make it their business or place to share their every opinion and nasty comment about other women? Why do women feel the need to disagree with what someone else feeds their kids? What sports or activities they sign their kids up for? Sometimes I feel like women can never measure up to other women's expectations. Now is the time to change all of that. Instead of putting a target on their backs and making them feel like shit, embrace a new perspective and believe that those other women are your equal, are doing their best, and do not need extra guilt or shame from you being added to her already overflowing plate.

The day I found out my mom was dying; I was blasting Eric Clapton's "Forever Man" in my car. I was alone, the sun was shining, and I was in a great mood. I looked at my screen and saw it was my dad. When I heard the words he shared, everything changed. It's taken me nearly two years to the day to be able to listen to that song without crying and feeling sick to my stomach. I have loved that song for years; it gives me energy, and I imagine myself hanging out with Eric (I know, I am such a cheese).

After that day, I was unable to listen to it. Just the other day, though, it was sunny out, and I started to think about the song and my mom (her birthday is coming up), and I cranked up "Forever Man," bopped my head, tapped my steering wheel, and sang my ass off. I chose to let go of the association I had with the memory of that day and the song. I think I'd felt guilty for a long time, like I wasn't respecting the event surrounding my mom. The things we do to ourselves, with those sorts of mind games!

I made the choice to take that experience and let it go. It was a conscientious decision. Why should I feel guilty about loving a song just because it was playing when I received some horrible news? I choose to celebrate the memories I have with my mom instead of attaching the sadness to it, knowing that it doesn't mean I have disrespected her or her memory. It doesn't lessen the love I have for her.

I have learned so much in the last decade about being a support, rather than an adversary, for other women. I have encountered women who have been so hurt by the words and actions of other ladies that they are incapable of believing another woman might not want the worst for them. To me, this is tragic. Women are so strong, so powerful, and our connections can be unbreakable when communication, trust, and respect are present in the relationship.

TOOLS:

As women, how can we cheer others on and make them feel valued, respected, and heard?

1. Give other women credit where credit is due. Hats off to their contributions to their community, their ideas in the workplace, and their accomplishments. Some women feel safe enough to share these things with friends and on social media, but far too often, other women bash them for "bragging" instead of being happy for them.

2. When you see another woman struggling, instead of judging her, ask how you can help.

3. If a woman is speaking, and you see or hear other women rolling their eyes with a "give me a break" look, shut them down.

4. It's time for all women to recognize that there is room in this universe for EVERYONE to succeed as themselves.

5. When you champion another woman for her ideas, creations, efforts, etc., you lose the weight of envy or judgement and feel lighter.

6. Be a leader and mentor for other women. If you are established in a business, *share what you know!* You remember how it felt to start from scratch, so don't be the person who fails to extend a hand to someone drowning.

THE MESSAGE:

- If you even think you are about to say something judgmental or mean about (or even to) another woman … think again. Stop yourself. Take a new approach and support her decision, whatever it is, because it's not yours to make. I mean, maybe she's having a bad week, maybe her kids are refusing to eat healthy snacks, and maybe she's just had it. What right or invitation do we have that makes us think it's okay to trash another woman?

CHAPTER THIRTEEN

WOMEN ARE MISUNDERSTOOD

Back when I was teaching, I had a friend who taught grade seven in the opposite wing of the school. He happened to be a guy, and we became fast friends as soon as we met. He was funny, good-looking, smart, and kind. Brian and I hung out a lot and spent a lot of time together. He was new to the area and had a girlfriend in another city. Although he had amazing qualities and characteristics, I wasn't attracted to him romantically. We drank and got silly and laughed our asses off, and I would crash in his spare room if I couldn't drive home from too many wobbly pops. His girlfriend eventually moved in with him, getting a teaching job at another school nearby, and they saved up to buy their first home. I really liked her; they made a great pair. The three of us got along well.

Brian would call me every day at four p.m. (often from the "throne") to chat about our days and how the junior-high kids were. It was a good way to end the day, chatting about any turds we had in our classes. The shape of the school meant we didn't see each other much during the day, so it was nice to chat. I was single and lived alone, so having someone who understood the pressures and frustrations of students was a welcomed feeling.

And then one day, I noticed the daily phone calls had stopped. I started to wonder if I had done something wrong. So, I finally asked him if he was mad at me. Brian paused and told me that Anna (now his fiancé) didn't want him to call me. I had also noticed that she'd seemed mad at me and wouldn't interact like she used to. What had I done? I finally got to the bottom of it.

Another teacher in our school had a wife who taught at the other school with Anna. She had been at our school and seen Brian and I joking around and chatting. She then took it upon herself to go back to her school and tell Anna that I obviously had feelings for Brian, and that she should "be careful."

My heart sank. What the hell? I loved him as a friend, but I'd never even entertained the thought of liking him more than that. Ever. I called Anna at her school and explained how sorry I was that she felt that way. I shared that I cared very much for Brian but that there had never been any sort of inappropriate feeling or anything between us, and never would be. But the damage had been done. She had become convinced that I was a threat to her relationship, and our friendship was forever frayed. Brian continued to be friendly at school, but we never did anything outside of work again.

I felt like I had lost one of my closest friends, and all because of a random woman who'd made it her mission to misconstrue and ruin a great friendship that I assume she didn't understand or have in her own life.

I was invited to Brian and Anna's wedding, and I happily attended. I had met his parents a few times before and thought they were lovely people. During the reception, I spoke with his father, and he leaned in and said, "Kiki, this must be hard for you. I'm glad you came!"

I thought, *Hard? What is he talking about?* "What do you mean hard? I'm having a great time! I had to save up to afford the hotel, but I'm so happy for them both."

He replied, "Well, we all know how much you like Brian and the feelings you have for him."

I was gutted. *What??? His family knows about this? They all think I have a crush on Brian?!* I had to get to the bottom of the nightmare quickly. I pulled Brian aside at one point and thanked him for inviting me to the wedding. While I apologized for bringing it up at his wedding, I told him that I hated the position I felt I had been put in.

"Brian, I just talked to your dad. Why does he think I like you? Do YOU think I have feelings for you?"

He paused. "Well, yeah, but it's okay, we can still be friends. I think you're great."

At that point I wanted to scream. Instead, I said, "Dude. I love ya, but not in that way. How could you think that and not say anything before now? I feel like I've been accused and convicted of feelings I don't even have!"

Although we chatted for a few more minutes, I knew I hadn't convinced him. I figured the only way to prove it was to distance myself from him and Anna. So, from that point on, I had essentially lost two wonderful friends, all thanks to an insecure, ill-meaning woman. I just wish this person would have had the ta-tas to come to me and ask before assuming the worst. How could a teacher (of all people) essentially bully another teacher? I saw her in a different light after that.

Has another woman created a situation about you based on feelings or actions that only existed in their mind? It baffles me that another woman would take it upon herself to create a major drama where there had been none at all! But women do this a lot, and some even thrive on creating drama, not only in other people's lives but their own as well. It's exhausting. Stay in your lane and try to understand where another woman is coming from, before assuming the worst and imagining and sharing a scenario (and drama) that doesn't exist.

TOOLS/THE MESSAGE:

- This is about looking at someone else's plight and minding your own business until you know the facts. Don't create drama in someone else's life; it's hard to undo the damage once you've done it, and it may not even be true. You've affected someone else's relationship in some way, and it's unfair and unnecessary. Seek to understand first before saying anything to anyone. Gossiping is nothing more than counterproductive and a waste of time and energy.

CHAPTER FOURTEEN

OUR BODIES AND THE MEDIA

Just when you thought you were starting to recognize and appreciate your body for all it does ... BAM! You get slapped in the face with tabloids, commercials, magazines, and criticism. It feels like you will never measure up or be good enough. We are bombarded with this crap on a daily basis. Advertisers know this, and get into our heads; it's how they make their money, with demeaning pictures of women, constantly promoting diet programs, surgeries, Botox, liposuction, boot camps, etc. When you see, hear, and experience it, our minds begin to believe it. This is precisely why we need to do the exact opposite when it comes to our bodies and how we see them. As women, we have to change our dialogue with ourselves, *and* each other.

As adults, we know where we get the messages from. But what about our children, who start to think their bodies aren't normal? Kids see it on social media and in magazines, and then there's cyber bullying as well. It's sad (but true) to think that women pass their own insecurities onto their kids. They might make a comment about another child in a dance group, hockey team, school play, etc. Our children LISTEN. They watch and they learn from us. Kids will move forward thinking it's okay to demean another child for their body, if they see or hear us doing the same, and they will begin to think that different body shapes and sizes are unacceptable. And that is WRONG! It leads to kids continuing the vicious circle of bullying and misconstrued messages that lead to body dysmorphia and eating disorders.

Thank God for women who are standing up and speaking out against this bullshit. Instagram leaders will show themselves as they are, crying and without makeup, breastfeeding their babies, running on the spot with jiggly legs, and then they show us poses that are typically used in the media. It's NOT normal to have completely clear, unblemished skin (hello, beauty industry!!) Today, in 2021, the beauty industry is valued in the hundreds of millions of dollars. This number is staggering! As female consumers, including girls as young as eleven, we are spending a phenomenal amount of money trying to look and feel better about ourselves. But are we spending it in the right places?

The diet industry alone is worth more than two billion dollars today. Taking a step back to assess the family and school dynamic over the past eighteen months, we absolutely must take a stand against the things we know are toxic. If we don't take care of ourselves, we are inviting disease and poor mental health to continue ruining our lives through the generations. We know better, so let's do better!

TOOLS:

1. Stand in front of the mirror. This may be scary for someone who has avoided the mirror for a long time. If you can find a full-length mirror, it's even better. Stand there naked. What do you see? How do you feel about your body? What words go through your mind? Are they encouraging or critical? If they are critical, what is it you're saying to yourself, and why? What makes you think that this part of your body doesn't measure up? And who are you measuring or comparing yourself to?

2. Inherently, we are born with a body that tells us when we are hungry, and the feeling of being full emerges when our bodies have had enough. Our bodies also crave fuel. Healthy, nutritious foods make our bodies function better, ultimately making us feel stronger emotionally, mentally, and physically. It's only when we allow external cues to guide us that we go off track, eat when we aren't hungry, starve our bodies, and see what isn't there. These issues begin when we try to find control in our lives and adopt all the inaccurate information coming from every angle.

3. While you are standing in the mirror, remember that your head is attached to your body. That may seem obvious, but you typically don't insult and abuse your head. Your head and your body are connected, so logically, think about all the things your body does for you. All the crevices and freckles and stretch marks, the scars and the blemishes. This body can run, leap, reach, and

carry. It can soothe, calm, and comfort another human being. This body is a miracle ... and so are you. If you have made a vow to your partner or made a silent vow to your child to love them unconditionally (along with your fur babies), you can make the same vow to yourself.

4. the following out loud to yourself, in front of that person in the mirror, many times throughout the day:

A. I will feed you nutritious fuel.

B. I will treat you with respect.

C. I will never criticize you again.

D. I will not judge or negatively comment on anyone's body, including my own.

E. I understand that bodies come in all shapes and sizes and each body is a miracle as it is.

F. I will never wish for someone else's body.

THE MESSAGE:

- Stop judging yourself! Do not compare your body with someone else's. They aren't you! Listen to your body's signals, and respect yourself enough to fuel your body with nutritious foods that will optimize how you feel, inside and out. Don't carry extra weight on your shoulders by knocking someone else down; that's the kind of ugliness no one needs to give ... or receive. And you're better than that. XO

CHAPTER FIFTEEN

WHAT DOES SHE HAVE THAT I DON'T?

Nothing, my beautiful friend. Nothing.

This is a commonly asked question when it comes to women comparing themselves to other women. What do you say to yourself when you see someone wearing a bikini that you wish you could wear? "My thighs are too jiggly" "OMG, I would never wear that, even if I did have her body!" What goes through your mind when you see someone driving your dream car? "Must be nice!" "Well, *I* don't have to drive an Escalade to prove *my* worth." How do you feel when you see someone wearing a diamond ring bigger than yours? When you meet someone who lives in a beautiful, big house and has another vacation house in the Caribbean or on a lake? Jealous? Envious? Do you wonder how they can afford these things, these luxuries, these *dreams* that you would like to have too?

First off, there's not a damned thing wrong with liking and/ or wanting more for yourself. I love shiny things, though it's a bit of a contrast to how I dress. I am usually in something from Smoothies, like a tank, sweatshirt, leggings, etc., and I'm almost always in flip flops or something casual (even though

I own more than two hundred pairs of shoes just in case the occasion calls for them). I feel most comfortable in cozy, casual clothes. I know other fabulous women who just don't feel like themselves unless they have make-up on and are always "put together."

I say, "Yay, for them!"

And I recognize class and beauty when I see it too. I could give two shits about the car you drive, or how big your house is. Truly. But my dreams and goals do include having a second house on a lake and quite possibly a home somewhere tropical and warm. And I happen to adore my 2.2 carat diamond engagement ring. Why should I apologize for driving an Escalade? I shouldn't. And I don't. It is a car. And my ring is just a ring. It does not define who I am, what I treasure/value, how I behave, or how deeply I feel or love. I started off with a $7,000 Hyundai Pony when my brother and I were in high school. I've worked hard to afford what I want.

I love to see other women succeed, win their dream home, build their dream home, drive their new Rolls Royce pickup (Who knew?!), or get pregnant. I feel nothing but happiness for them. I almost feel like I am part of their excitement! My friend and her husband sold their young company for more than five million dollars. My first reaction was to call and scream my excitement into the phone. I thought of how it would change their lives and how their finances would be less of a stress, giving them more of an opportunity to grow it elsewhere.

I know that the universe holds so much incredible energy and abundance that, if I want something, I can go get it; it's already there in the realm of the universe. I have to change how I approach it, however. It's one thing to want something, and quite another to manifest it.

Women have been taught to hustle and "make it happen." I've used that phrase countless times throughout my life; my dad taught me that. He (a man) is physiologically different from me (a woman with more estrogen). His masculine energy requires that he be a "doer," a provider. As a female, I hold more feminine energy, and that is to receive. One of the most difficult things about being a woman is undoing the expectations of masculine energy. We don't have to hustle constantly to make things happen.

What does that mean to someone who wants to start a business, or improve her relationship, or create more wealth in her life?

It means we need to be specific about what we want. And when we know it for sure, we can set about changing our energy towards it. We all have subconscious energies that have programmed and coded us throughout our lives. Because we don't necessarily always think about those memories and experiences and how they affected us, we try to stay in the conscious side of things and think about what we want now. We dream about the house, the relationship, the trip, the baby, the money, etc. So how do we create the things we want in our lives?

Trust and surrender.

That is no small feat, my friends. How do we let go of the fear, ridicule, expectations, judgements, failures, programming?

You have to learn how to quiet your mind long enough to identify what is blocking you from having the things you want and achieving the goals you've set.

Remember, it's all there. When you think about that woman who has the things and people in her life that you would love to have … she is no better than you. She wasn't given a universal pass to succeed. She recognized what she wanted, and she allowed herself to RECEIVE everything she wanted. I used to get caught up in the HOW. I would set goals like making $40,000 in sales in a month and then start sweating bullets: How would I make that happen? What would I do? I would get so worked up about it that I inevitably pushed it away. Think about a butterfly, for example. They are beautiful creatures, and we often chase them. Do you ever notice what happens when you chase a butterfly? It flutters away from you. Have you ever tried standing or sitting still and quiet? So many times, I have stopped chasing, and that butterfly begins to come closer to me. I get excited about it, but if I stay still and admire its captivating nature, it often lands right on me. I've allowed myself to RECEIVE its presence and grace.

That's what anxiety is. We freak out about the what ifs, how, when, where etc. We either create more fear inside of a situation that we have no control over and have to accept, or we end up repelling what we want to attract.

I watch and study women who are successful, empowered, kind, and influential. (While I try to stay away from the comparison, it sometimes creeps in.) How did they get an interview on TV? How is their product better than mine? Why haven't I made $2 million in sales this year? Why isn't it happening? How will I make that happen?

I must stop and think about what hasn't worked in the past and recognize that my subconscious only wants me to be safe. And I am.

So, I need to let go of the fears and insecurity, meditate, quiet my mind, and surrender to what the universe is giving me.

Every morning (well okay, almost), I look in the mirror and I (try to) smile. I tell myself these things: "I am sorry. I forgive you. I love you. Thank you."

Then I open my bathroom cupboard door and read these affirmations out loud:

1. I let go of what no longer serves me.
2. I release all limiting beliefs.
3. I release self-doubt.
4. I let go of fear.
5. I release attachment to outcome.
6. I release toxic friendships.
7. I let go of relationships that no longer serve my highest good (not easy for many women).
8. I let go of worry.
9. I release lack and know that the universe is abundant.

10. I let go of negativity.

11. I release all that is not in alignment with my life path.

Then I read the following statements, which serve me personally and are effective first thing in the morning, out loud:

1. I live mindfully and eat mindfully.

2. The past does not control me.

3. I give my body permission to change.

4. I release all guilt and shame around food and my body.

5. Happiness is not size-specific.

6. I am abundant.

7. I am doing my best, and that is enough.

8. There is no need to binge since I have unconditional permission to eat.

This forces me to re-program for the day. I try to stretch and wake my body up. When I stretch slowly, it allows me to recognize that my body is part of me. I don't separate its existence from "me," and allow myself to treat it poorly, because that would mean not loving ME. I used to eat mindlessly, eating very fast, and not even having the pleasure of tasting the food and enjoying the textures. I was feeding the void, not nourishing my body. And to be honest, every damn day is a new beginning. I'm just like millions of you out there who start a program and veer off course. So, I gain my strength and determination and start again. And I'm okay with that.

Remember the vibrational cone we talked about earlier? I just couldn't understand why things were not happening for me (why I couldn't lose weight, make huge sales like other women-owned companies, etc.). Then I learned about my energy and my subconscious.

I was operating on a very low vibration, with anxiety, shame, and guilt being always at the forefront of my mind. I carried these emotions with me, and it's a miracle I operated at all. However, the breakthrough here is showing me how resilient and strong I am as a woman. I functioned like I was at a medium or high frequency, and yet I was almost always at the lower end. That caused a lot of frustration from within, because I desperately wanted to be a happy, "see the glass as half full" kind of person. But I could not get out of my own way long enough to allow myself to let go and receive. I felt I wasn't deserving or worthy of it. In fact, growing up, I just figured I was someone who would never truly be happy or feel content. I seemed to search for more all the time, but I know it was a need I had created based on how I interpreted my experiences and worth (or lack of it) to be.

Over the years, I have watched and learned from other women. I know that millions of us carry burdens far beyond the lessons they were meant to bring. It's that masculine energy projecting itself into our thought processes. We must suffer for our sins (so to speak). We must continue to beat ourselves up for an event that took place in our past. Don't forget that we are defined by how we respond to those experiences, not what happened. Why is it that when a man cheats on us, we blame ourselves? I must have done something for him to act this way. I must be a bad partner if he felt he needed to be with someone else. "I made my bed, and now I must lie in it." Ummmm … No you don't, sister! You have every friggin right in this world to make a choice. And although many women stay in relationships for their children, I don't know that it serves anyone involved to do that. Kids pick up on the resentment and tension in your relationship. They feel it too. But that's a decision you must make, based on your life. I will not judge you, because it's what *you* would do … not necessarily what I would do. I couldn't live with someone who did that, because I know *myself* well enough to know it would eat *me* up inside daily, and that trust would be non-existent.

Do you know yourself well? Do you know what triggers your fears, your anxiety? What brings you joy? What blocks you from taking the risks necessary to bring about the change you want to see in your life? What brings tears of sadness and pain? What do you envision when you think of the perfect day? Vacation? Job? What are your passions? Think about those things for a minute.

Knowing yourself is key when it comes to manifesting your desires. I know I am a water sign because I've been drawn to it my entire life. My spaces are typically surrounded by pieces of artwork, décor, and even scents of the ocean. Shells, glass, etc. are a constant reminder of who I am at my core and how I feel safe and secure. It's why I think I am more of a homebody than anything else. I have painted walls that represent soothing and calm. I have open spaces that reflect the open, vast sea. That's what I'm talking about when I say you really need to know yourself. What speaks to you? What is it *you* need?

I'm not a great routine person; I get bored easily, so I am trying something new. Each morning when I wake up, I figure out what I will need for myself that day. How much time will I dedicate to myself? Self-care is also self-love. When we put off exercise, journaling, stretching, taking a luxurious bath, etc., we are saying to ourselves that we don't love ourselves enough to take the time our bodies and minds need to function at our highest level. In fact, most of the women I know and read about are merely existing. We know that we put others before ourselves, and I've said it before, but it truly is a statement that you're making to and about yourself: I don't love or respect myself enough to take the time I require to be whole. And believe me, when you put that kind of statement out there, other people feed off that, and then *they* don't respect or love you the way you deserve either!

Some activities that bring me joy and gratitude are journaling, stretching, walking in nature, walking on the beach, being outside, meditating, Yin yoga, and listening to music. When I go to sleep at night, I always put on ocean sounds. It lulls me to sleep, and I love it. My son Kristopher does the same (I think it might be because he wants to be like his mom, but I'll take it!). I just came across a YouTube channel with sounds meant to create a melatonin effect, helping you to fall asleep faster.

It's lovely, really. (Search "Fall Asleep in Under 3 MINUTES * Body Mind Restoration * Melatonin Release)

I am at my best when I can help others. I know this. I am a nurturer. I want to bring about change for girls and women, so we stop this insane cycle of self-destructive behaviours. Women are now leaders of empires, talk shows, and media corporations, and we are tired of taking that back seat. Encourage each other to take a leap of faith and follow your gut. That's hard when you don't trust yourself, so go back to the three important characteristics of any relationship: Communication, Trust, Respect.

I don't pretend to think that I never screw up, make a decision based on fear, or react instead of reflecting. I am human and will continue to do and say things I might later say, *Hmmmmmm, not the best reaction, Kiki.* But I can learn from it and move on. It's all I can do because I am finished holding on to those things. Life is too short, isn't it? I mean, do you really think we were meant to be on this earth to demean ourselves, gain weight and hate ourselves, judge each other, and become shells of the person we should be? NO. It is something I must think about each day, if I am going to achieve what I want in this life.

I also know what I stand for.

TOOLS:

1. Know what brings you accessible joy and fulfillment.
   Write them down and practice doing them each week.

Allow yourself to enjoy those moments, free of guilt and distractions.

2. Once you can eke out that time, you'll not only appreciate that space, but you'll respect yourself more for claiming your power. This increases confidence and your belief in yourself and creates more energy for you to share with the people you love most …other than yourself, of course!

THE MESSAGE:

- If we refuse to take a stand on claiming time and space just for us, we slowly start to break down. We are unbelievably strong, but it takes courage, and your voice, to let others know you believe in yourself.

- Now that I have created Smoothies Tank Tops, as a brand that believes in empowerment, I have made decisions to stand up for those beliefs.

CHAPTER SIXTEEN

SMOOTHIES TANK TOPS: BECOMING AN ENTREPRENEUR

"Athleisure is a marriage of athletic wear and the new (here to stay) trend to be comfortable and confident in who you are and what you wear every day."

— Kiki Rozema

Although starting a business and becoming an entrepreneur has been a part of my journey, I realize that many of you might have no interest in doing this yourself. And that's okay! While this chapter offers some advice on doing so, and lessons I learned along the way, I believe there are little snippets of wisdom here and there that could be helpful in your life no matter *what* your next goals or plans might be. So, please bear with me while I talk to those who *are* interested in it and see if any of the advice might resonate with you as well.

(What have you got to lose?)

If you are planning to start your own business, take the time to establish your values and how you will integrate them into the company.

Women seem to want to reinvent themselves, and not only is starting your own business possible but more and more women are doing it and becoming quite successful. I know I have products that are amazing in several ways, so why shouldn't I also be one of those success stories? Why shouldn't YOU?

Knowing where your talents and passions lie is important when it comes to business. You want to embark on a career that brings you joy and profit. It's not okay to assume all women want to work, but there's been an increase in the number of women who do. Historically, women have been placed in the home, caring for children (their own and others). There are women who thoroughly enjoy it, and others who need something different to fill their bucket. It can be a scary thing to get out into the workforce, reinvent yourself as an entrepreneur, and be successful. We've had to fight for equal pay and respect in the typically male world of business.

Childcare providers expend an extraordinary amount of energy and care for our children; it's incredible how little they are actually paid. But as we all know, the price of childcare can prevent us from going back into the workforce altogether. More women are trying to go back to work for more than just financial reasons; we are becoming more aware of our need to interact with adults, utilize our talents and passions, and do something for ourselves. In generations past, women not only wanted but were expected to marry, bear children, and keep a happy, clean home. But now we need emancipation from the chains of society. The roadblocks still include unequal pay and being undervalued.

Allow me to reassure you. Your worth is the value you place within yourself. If you command respect and equal pay, we begin to change how women are treated, rather than accepting the former roles we were once accustomed to.

Women are starting to take a bigger role in entrepreneurship across North America, Not only is this inspiring for women who are interested in starting their own business, but it also presents the opportunity to build a stronger economy.

In the summer of 2018, my family and I were making the twelve-hour drive to British Columbia to go boating for two weeks. As always, I wore a tank top underneath my t-shirt, and even though I was sitting in the car doing nothing, my tank was riding up. It was putting me over the edge with frustration. *Why* did every single one of my tanks do this? I wore a tank for a few reasons. For example, I wanted to cover up the cellulite on my tummy, and psychologically, I felt I was "covered" if I had that layer.

My mind began to spin: THIS is how I could help millions of women who have the same issue! I reflected on how many women I saw pulling their tanks down and constantly having to readjust. It had to frustrate them too! And I wasn't the only overweight woman who wore tanks as a layer, as well as a workout top.

There were a few issues I needed to address. I knew zip about business. I had never run my own company before and knew nothing about fabrics and manufacturing. Nada. Zilch. ZERO.

Being able to teach a classroom of hormonal teenagers successfully had certainly begun to boost my confidence. I drew on that experience to remind myself that I was capable of not only making a difference for women with my apparel but of running a thriving company as well.

It almost came to me as an epiphany; I had spent years helping students, wanting to help females, and dealing with my own issues that were prevalent among others. I could start my own company with the foundation and principles of helping girls and women feel more confident about who they are and what they wore. That was in August 2018.

I made my first phone call in November 2018 to manufacturers in Canada (I felt it was important to have all our products made here), and I began researching textile companies also in Canada. I was very honest and upfront about my lack of knowledge and asked these companies to help me in narrowing down the best fabrics. I learned about the manufacturing process and production times. I researched other athleisure brands and how they'd started, who the CEO/Founders were, and how they marketed their brands. What did their websites look like? Was I going to be an online store or get into physical retail stores? Or both?

We aren't just a Tank Top company trying to sell tanks. Our tank tops are literally designed to make you feel more confident.

After going through over a hundred samples of fabric, I found what I thought would be the best possible fabric for our tanks. They have a smooth outside and a brushed, super soft interior, that prevented the tank from riding up. I am a huggy person and did research on the psychological effects of hugging someone. Did you know that when you hug someone for more than five seconds, it raises oxytocin (the happy hormone) and lowers cortisol (the stress hormone)? I designed the tanks to be fitted; the fabric has this amazing stretch that doesn't lose its shape, and being so soft, it really did feel like a hug.

Wearing it, I felt like I was no longer vulnerable. I was put together. The straps are substantial, so the girls aren't flopping out all over the place, and it covers the areas that drove me (and our customers) crazy. They are longer, to cover the butt and lower abdomen. The fabric is non-see-through, so even if I wear mine on its own, I don't feel like my cellulite is exposed. I feel good about myself and my body when I wear our tanks, and I wear one every single day, because I feel naked if I don't. It feels sort of like a second skin, and without yanking it down all the time, you forget it's on … you just feel better about yourself. The fitted nature and the fabric allow our tanks to smooth you out, rather than sucking you in. I'd say that's a lot of punch for a tank top!

As it turns out, I was right about our tank tops filling a need for women; thousands of women have purchased our tanks and absolutely LOVE them! I am proud to say we have only had four returns in two and a half years in business. I'd say that's amazing, and I'm proud to share that.

It wasn't enough to design tank tops though. We've got eco-friendly leggings, sweats, and tops, all made with women's shapes, sizes, and feelings in mind. I began to think I should expand the company, so Smoothies Tank Tops is now a size-inclusive, athleisure brand. Our tanks range in size from small to 4XL, and our leggings go from small to 3XL. And I've just introduced our self-care line, making it even simpler for us to take care of ourselves. I've branded my own body creams, soaps, wine tumblers (yes, wine is self-care!) and taller tumblers with lids/straws. We also carry a totally eco-friendly, organic and wildcrafted facewash and cream, owned by a former student who now runs her own company called Blink Botanicals!

I want to help women not only through our apparel but also the resources we have developed. Our private Facebook group, Confidence Connection, allows women to speak their minds and share their experiences without feeling judged or belittled. When we are supported by other women, we can change the dynamics of our relationships and the stigma around sensitive female issues.

I started the Empowerment/Mentorship Camp for Girls so we could bring about change in how girls view and feel about themselves and where they fit into this constantly changing world. I want them to make these changes before they turn thirty and ask how they could have allowed their hatred for themselves to grow, instead of the gratitude and appreciation they need to flourish as young women.

Our camp is three days; we greet the girls with a welcome package full of special items like a Smoothies Tank Top, journal, pen, a welcome letter from their mentor, and a camp t shirt. We have a stacked itinerary with team building, physical movement, journal writing, yoga, meditation, guest speakers, crafts, fireside chats, and true camaraderie. We have discussions on bullying, female friendships, our choices, acceptance, and more. It's very powerful, and our campers seem to love it! Our second camp is September 2021.

At fifty-two years old, I have finally concluded that I am a good, worthy human being. I find it interesting that I have gone my whole life believing I wasn't good enough, that I wasn't worthy of someone genuinely loving me for me. That feeling of being broken had followed me everywhere. I interpreted the words and actions of others to determine my path. As I've said before, we are our beliefs and mindset. I knew I was intelligent, but when it came to my career, I thought maybe I didn't measure up. I had to prove my worth by enrolling in a master's degree program. Once I graduated, I wanted more for myself.

As I've said, when I decided to start my own company, I knew zip about running a business. Marketing, numbers, and business was never something I had thought about. I literally flew by the seat of my pantaloons for the first nine months. I had to sit down and write out all the things I thought I would need to do to start. It was incredibly overwhelming, but I had a purpose. Just as I wanted to make a difference in teaching, I knew there was something to be said about making millions of women feel good about who they were and helping them learn how to love their bodies once again. If you are one of the few women out there who has gratitude and respect for your body as it is, I applaud you, and I am hugging you right now! Seriously, that is incredible. And at the same time, isn't it sad to imagine that there are so few women out there who feel good about themselves?

It takes a Herculean effort today to overcome the ridicule, expectations, and pressures of just being female.

Owning a company means you're not only invested financially but also emotionally. I take people's comments to heart, and my aim is to provide superior customer service. I will replace or exchange a garment, should there be an issue. I return emails and messages within hours, but often within minutes. I want women to know that there is another woman out there who cares about how they feel, and that I understand their pain points when it comes to clothing. I believe that what we wear reflects how we feel. If I'm wearing something constricting and/or scratchy, it makes my skin crawl. Now that we have weathered the Covid storm, we can appreciate the comforts of home and the apparel that makes us feel our best. It's why I only design clothing that fits, flatters, and functions.

A while back, I looked on social media and saw someone remark on an ad my team had placed on Facebook. She said something along the lines of "Well I guess these are supposed to be great, but that was a baller move, asking me to write you a review when I haven't even received my order yet. I know you are having shipping delays, but seriously. Just sayin'."

Back story: We have grown as a company, and because of that, I decided to ship all my inventory to British Columbia to a distribution center. As a result, there were some major delays in costumers getting their orders. Like a month's delay. I am a very impatient person, and this would drive me crazy too. I took the time to email every customer who had placed their order within the last five weeks. I explained what had happened, that I appreciated their business and loyalty in our company, and that I would offer a 20 percent discount on their next order as a thank you. I felt it was necessary to be honest in terms of what was happening, so people didn't lose respect or hope in our company. I had to reassure them their next order would be shipped out within twenty-four hours of them placing it.

So, when I saw this comment, a few things went through my mind: Why would she air her grievance on my social-media account? It has nothing to do with the positivity of the ad or what we stand for as a brand. Is she trying to stir up shit? Did she think it would make her order ship out faster? I felt it made us look bad, while I was bending over backwards to make the customer experience a good one. In fact, I'd gone above and beyond by sending fifty customers a facial mask, as a token of my appreciation and a reminder for self-care. I deleted her comment and emailed her. I asked her to please refrain from sharing her apparent disappointment on social media, asking her to please email us with any concerns she may have so we can address them in an appropriate way. She then went to another ad we had and posted something like this: "I got your disrespectful email. If you can't handle a joke on social media, maybe you shouldn't have it. You have lost my business." I sat back and reflected. So, I did a "baller move" and called her. She didn't answer, so I left a voicemail in a pleasant and cheery voice:

"Hi, Leann. It's Kiki from Smoothies. I saw your second comment on Facebook; thanks for that. I'm not interested in any more issues, and it appears you're not the kind of customer who values our aims at making a positive difference for women, so I've cancelled your order and given you a full refund. Thanks so much, take care."

You can't win everyone over, but I feel my response was professional and honest. For some people though, that just isn't enough! So, you move on, knowing you did your best.

No more drama.

Now some people might say that was a silly thing to do. I'd just lost a customer. I disagree. I had removed someone who was out to be a nuisance, and felt they had a right to be an idiot in my space. No thanks.

As the leader of Smoothies, I must be the voice of the women who want change. Women who want to know and feel their worth, who want to learn how to do better for themselves so they can show up for others. Everyone is welcome to be a part of the Smoothies family. But if you can't play nicely in the sandbox, you get a permanent time-out. That is how I will protect my brand, my efforts, and the other women who are as bound and determined as I am to make that change for others.

When you find a retreat, book, mentor, coach, or whatever that can help you recognize your greatness, you take the bull by the horns, utilize your "masculine" energy, and sign up!!

Don't use your fear as a vehicle for resisting change, putting off your well-deserved happiness! It just doesn't make sense.

But you will be tested.

As we move forward in our lives and ask for more from the universe, we are going to face more challenges. When I thought I would be single forever, I focused on myself, and the right man appeared. When we wanted a child and had miscarriages and failed adoptions, I wanted to give up at times. I thought maybe God was telling me I wasn't meant to be a mom. Those were the times when I was emotionally drained from loss and disappointment. But inherently, I do believe I had a lot of love to share and give a baby, so I didn't understand why it was happening. I look back and recall the agony and anxiety I endured daily, wondering if we would ever hold our baby and become parents. Now that my children are four and eight, I see that everything happens when it is supposed to, and all the angst and energy I expended wasn't necessary after all. When we can trust the universe and surrender to what it has to offer, the anxiety falls away, and we are lighter and happier. When I moved all my Smoothies inventory to British Columbia (fourteen hours away), and they took over five weeks to get orders shipped out, I wondered if I had made a huge mistake with my company and the distribution company. Was this a sign that I should fold my company?

The distribution company I hired had a system that was confusing to me, and through the dozens of emails, it became apparent that it would take way longer than I had anticipated for these orders to get out. I would watch the numbers on Shopify stay the same for hours and days at a time. My anxiety started to grow, and I panicked. I hated having customers wait for their orders. I want them to get their order quickly and efficiently, and this was excruciating. I tried calling the company to speak to someone who could help walk me through the process and make it happen faster. Ultimately, Neil drove to B.C. and retrieved everything, bringing it all back to Alberta. We re-stocked our inventory, and when necessary, I will get a warehouse a lot closer to home!

This is where I must remind myself that getting worked up about something won't solve the issue. It's just going to frustrate me and cause anxiety. I remind myself that what defines me is how I respond to the situation. I literally had to stop myself and breathe in and out. A few times.

If I was going to grow the company, I couldn't give up. It was the universe testing me and seeing what I was made of. Do I really want this to succeed? How will I respond to adverse situations? How will I handle hiccups when they (inevitably) occur? We have to think about this like a video game when you are climbing success levels: Things get harder, we lose our player, get points, lose points, and then work our way to the next level, with a new player. But if we want to get to that next level, we keep playing. And if the frustration gets to us, we walk away briefly and then come back to try again. It's okay to give yourself a time-out to regroup. What draws us back to our idea (for a business) is not only the passion to get better but the purpose and values you place on it.

Today, Smoothies Tank Tops is two and a half years old. For half of that time, the world has been on various degrees of lockdown with the Covid-19 pandemic. Everyone everywhere has been affected in one way or another. I had so many losses, I wasn't sure if I should tank the company or keep going. I did question myself about the difference I was making. I looked at my sales the first year compared to the current year, and although they'd more than doubled, I felt I needed to get out of the starting gate and make a name for myself in the industry.

Athleisure is terribly competitive, so how was I going to stand out from everyone else who had been in business much longer and were already established?

I took my entire life's experiences, how the relationship with my mom affected me, my weight, my belief system, my teaching career, and who I had become to get resourceful.

I had to be me. It had taken me more than three decades to figure out who the hell I really was and who I wanted to be. If I could be me—authentically *me*—I could be different than anyone else. I knew what it was like to feel uncomfortable in my clothing. I used to get red lines around my waistline when I wore jeans, because companies only manufactured jeans that were curvy. My waist hurt every second of the day, and my jeans were baggy in the thighs and arse. I felt fat ALL the time, because I didn't fit the mold society and fashion had decided on. It SUCKED. To this day, I still buy jeans, hoping they will look good. Ummmmm ... I look like a fifty-two-year-old wearing diapers. It's still the same, except now that spandex has entered the scene, the waist stretches out, and if I sneeze, my jeans end up around my ankles. Super attractive!

I've found it brutal to try and keep up with the millennials on social media; it takes up way too much of my time, and the push seems to be more on adding followers and likes and less on brand awareness and sales. I want to get our message across North America, because body image and lack of confidence is a global issue.

Thanks to inequality in the workplace, and social and cultural biases, women have been in the backseat far too long. We have carried the burdens of domestic duties, working full time, having side gigs, and caring for everyone but ourselves. When we are told to exercise SELF-CARE, most of us don't have a clue what that means. When would we have time for ourselves? How am I expected to practice yoga with toddlers and dogs hanging off me?

Confidence means taking the bull by the horns and making it happen. We *do* have the time; we just have to prioritize and claim that time for ourselves. Self-preservation means knowing when you've had enough instead of ignoring the physical signs of becoming worn out. And *not* apologizing for needing and wanting that time and space.

Smoothies Tank Tops has always been more than just a tank, both literally and figuratively. Our tanks fit and function like no other, and our brand includes clothing and self-care products that remind you to *take care of yourself* and *love being you* ... a little more each day.

We will continue to design clothing that flatters all figures and feels incredible against your skin. And we pledge to create and carry high-quality, low earth-impact self-care products for women.

The global market is expected to reach $546 million by 2024. (Allied Market Research titled: Activewear market) It's clear that stiff suits and uncomfortable, scratchy clothing for work has had its day. We are moving on!

But it doesn't seem to matter what kind of business you are in, when social media is involved (which it always is these days), you truly have to take a step back from the noise and remember your WHY.

I feel like I should mention this: Don't start a business for the money. Clearly you want to make profit, but the most successful companies are the ones that want to make a difference for others. The money seems to be a by-product of whatever you value as a company, how you will solve a problem for the customer, how you will respond when things go wrong, your customer experience, and standing up for your core values.

There is absolutely no way you will appease every single person out there, but we have to incorporate Facebook, Instagram, and other avenues to get our brands out there and grab the attention of as many people as possible. The issue, sometimes, is when people are behind a screen and throw out arbitrary comments. When you've put your heart and soul into your business and spent crazy amounts of money branding your company, paying people for ads, website design, manufacturing your goods, arranging, and building your business ... it can hurt.

I recently had someone comment on an ad we placed on Facebook about how I must not want "fat" people to be seen in photos (because that particular image didn't have a model who was a 3XL or bigger). I took that as an insult for several reasons. First, I am a plus-size person, so what's with the "fat people" reference? I also work tirelessly to get designs and programs out there to make a difference for women. Talk about judging a book by its cover! Our website showcases women of all different ethnicities, heights, sizes, and hair and eye color. This woman took one look at one picture and just assumed that ours was another company out there that claimed to be size inclusive but didn't really value those things. I suppose I would be just as offended if I was a service-based business.

Passion and being true to your values will help you to plow through all the tests you will be given throughout your journey. And just when you think one thing has been accomplished, another challenge will present itself. Business owners have a lot of pressure to be the captain of the ship and to make the decisions that best serve the company. When you are a woman in her fifties, just keeping track of your marbles is a task in and of itself some days.

If you don't know what I'm talking about, it's perimenopause. It's bad enough that we get our periods every month for years, bringing with it mood swings, emotional outbursts, cramping, etc., but then we have to put up with an entirely new set of (unwanted) issue. I feel like I am losing my mind a bit more every day! My husband will ask me about something I was supposed to do a week before and not only did I forget to do the thing, but I forgot he even asked me to do it at all. I'm talking about having no recollection whatsoever. That's scary!

And while I am grieving the loss of my brother, and trying to run my company alone, I will find myself crying for no apparent reason. And I'll look at my husband and think, *Do I really like you right now?* And the poor guy has done *nothing* wrong! I thought maybe it was just the stress of the things happening in my life, but when I researched it, I discovered that I was experiencing a lot of the symptoms commonly referred to as "the change of life." UGH. So, if you have mood swings, brittle nails, memory loss, anxiety, depression, achy joints, and irregular periods ... this could be the reason why. Reach out to your girlfriends and let them know they aren't on a "day-pass." It's just part of the joys of being a woman!

Life throws things at us all the time. Do you ever feel like you have "made it" and then things fall apart? Like someone or something is out to get you? Like why is this happening to me? I've learned a lot about how I respond to situations when they occur, and it really is the defining moment for us and who we are. Our subconscious tells us, "I told you so," and we revert back to the memories and beliefs we had in the past. But if we stay in that mindset, we never get ahead. Have you heard people tell you that there are lessons to be learned while in supposed crisis mode? It's true. You may not know what the lessons are right away; in fact, you may never be aware of these lessons. But living a life means we learn and evolve.

When you dream about those things in life you'd like to have, and then something happens where you start to question if maybe you weren't meant to have them, or think that you must not deserve them, NOW is the time to put on your big-girl panties and say, "SCREW THIS. Not only am I worthy of this but I want it and am going to go get it!"

TOOLS:

Take a few things into considering when starting a new business:

1. Is this something you're doing for the money or as a passion?
2. What problem are you solving for the consumer?
3. How much money will you need to start out?
4. Is this an online store, a home-based business, or brick and mortar?
5. Do you bring any experience to the business?

THE MESSAGE:

- I truly believe we can do anything we want. I spent more than $100,000 acquiring three degrees to become a teacher. I left after fifteen years, because my administrator didn't agree with my needing to work part-time to start a family. His beliefs didn't align with mine, and because my family was more of a priority, I had to leave. When I was ready, the ideas came to me, and at forty-nine, I started my own company. These things are doable! I began my company with $7000. You have to believe in who you are and what you want to accomplish in the business, and the rest you can learn along with way. Ask questions and do your research; it's all there.

CHAPTER SEVENTEEN

TODAY

"Wellness isn't just a state of mind. It's now a state of fashion."

— Kiki Rozema

Covid-19 has brought about a great deal of change; it's brought to the forefront the need for wellness from within ourselves and the environment. It's not enough to say we need to take time for ourselves; now is the time for action. People want to share, on social media, the steps they're taking to drink more water, wear clothing made with safe and healthy manufacturing practices, demonstrate healthy emotional/mental exercises, etc. The last eighteen months has been a wakeup call, a smack-in-your-face taste of reality about what we need to be grateful for. Our health is all we have, and if you don't have that, what success is there to celebrate?

Life can be taken away quickly. It's not okay to be indifferent about your health and wellness. If you've taken a break from being good to yourself, start again. Your mind and body will welcome you back with open arms and a sense of relief.

THIS IS NOW.

Shit or get off the pot.

I hope you have read this book and were able to reflect on some things in your life. I hope the perspective you once had has been shifted for the better, so you can see things through a different lens and possibly change the path you were heading down.

Finding my confidence and recognizing my success took time and trusting that things were going to work out for me. I wanted to share my experiences with you so that you would have an insider's glance at how I arrived at being me; how we can start a new career at any age; and that, when it comes right down to it, our passion for healthy change needs to override our fears.

If you are a woman reading this, I can almost guarantee you have felt some of the emotions and experienced some of these circumstances at some point throughout your life.

Making changes in our lives isn't always the easiest thing to do. We are comfortable doing what we have always done, but if we want a different result, we must go through the pain, anxiety, and fear of the unknown and learn to trust the universe as a whole, accepting that even though things may not be how you pictured them, there are lessons to be learned (however painful and unfair they seem to be at the time), and that, if we do our part to make the path clearer, we'll find the opportunities that are already waiting for us.

I hope that reading this book is a wakeup call for you—as writing it was for me—to take better care of yourself, physically, mentally, and emotionally. Even if all you want is to serve others, you must take care of *you* first.

There may not be a tomorrow, so take the time to make even the smallest change in your life. I know you can do it. I am working hard to do this myself. So instead of sitting on the couch after dinner, I am walking at night. I stretch. I look in the mirror and tell myself that it's my birthright to be happy. I try to find the joy in the small things instead of focusing on what annoys me, like when my four-year-old whines relentlessly. I try not to weigh myself too often, and instead I gauge my weight by how my clothes fit; it brings about too many feelings of disappointment if I'm constantly on the scale, so not measuring my worth or success by a number on the scale saves me from going off the rails entirely.

I've included a few of my own affirmations below so that you can see what has been working for me. Clearly, you know what triggers you and what your pain points are, so maybe these will help you, or at least, give you an idea for wording that might resonate with you more strongly.

Let's work together to change how we feel about ourselves. Let's become more connected with our bodies and nurture the relationships which serve us best. If you do not really like yourself, it shows. And you can only fool yourself and others for so long before the jig is up, and you feel like a fraud. Don't forget that you can reinvent yourself at any time, so take those small steps toward doing just that. You, and everyone who matters to you, will thank and respect you for it!

I am committed to growing Smoothies Tank Tops and what we offer, so that women know there is a company doing its best to open the doors for other women, to cheer them on and lift them up. Be present in your thoughts and actions and remind yourself of the greatness you are and how exceptional you can be.

I wish you every success!

Kiki

I am abundant

YOU ARE Beautiful

BE THE LEADER
YOU WOULD FOLLOW

Your past shapes
who you are
***
What defines you is
how you respond
to those
experiences

**I no longer hold onto
guilt, fear or shame,
because it doesn't serve me**

I am worthy of forgiveness

I release all guilt and shame
around food and my body

CPSIA information can be obtained
at www.ICGtesting.com
Printed in the USA
BVHW092136100422
633153BV00003B/11